Anonymous

**The Apostolic Age Young Men's Mutual Improvement Associations Manual**

Anonymous

**The Apostolic Age Young Men's Mutual Improvement Associations Manual**

ISBN/EAN: 9783337404253

Printed in Europe, USA, Canada, Australia, Japan

Cover: Foto ©Lupo / pixelio.de

More available books at **www.hansebooks.com**

# YOUNG MEN'S

# MUTUAL IMPROVEMENT ASSOCIATIONS

# MANUAL.

1898-9.

SUBJECT:
THE APOSTOLIC AGE.

## OFFICERS OF THE GENERAL SUPERINTENDENCY.

WILFORD WOODRUFF, General Superintendent.
JOSEPH F. SMITH, }
HEBER J. GRANT, } Counselors.
B. H. ROBERTS, }

### BOARD OF AIDS.

FRANCIS M. LYMAN,         EDWARD H. ANDERSON,
JOHN HENRY SMITH,         DOUGLAS M. TODD,
MATTHIAS F. COWLEY,       JOHN E. HEPPLER,
ABRAHAM O. WOODRUFF,      EDWARD H. SNOW,
J. G. KIMBALL,            NEPHI L. MORRIS,
JUNIUS F. WELLS,          RICHARD W. YOUNG,
MILTON H. HARDY,          HORACE G. WHITNEY,
RODNEY C. BADGER,         WM. S. BURTON,
GEO. H. BRIMHALL,         WILLARD DONE.

THOMAS HULL, - - Secretary and Treasurer
EVAN STEPHENS, - - - - Musical Director.

## INTRODUCTION.

*To Officers and Members:*

DEAR BRETHREN: We heartily congratulate you on the great revival of interest in Mutual Improvement work during the past season, and especially on the thorough and efficient work done by you on the course of study outlined in the Manual for 1897-8. We feel that our anticipations in these respects have been realized. The wisdom of limiting the work to one main subject, and making that subject THE LIFE OF JESUS, has been fully vindicated. We feel most grateful to you for the earnest and faithful labors you have performed in thus advancing the great work of Mutual Improvement.

In presenting to you the Manual for 1898-9, we have been mindful of the success you have achieved in the study of the preceding one, and have therefore determined to prescribe but one main subject for your study. There was only one opinion in the committee meeting as to what that subject should be. Our unanimous choice, after due consideration, was THE APOSTOLIC AGE. Following, as it does, the brief period of Christ's ministry, and taking up the work where He laid it down, it seemed to us the logical subject to follow the narrative of His life and labor. Like the course of study you have already taken, it affords ample opportunity for cultivating an understanding of the principles of the Gospel. Herein consists one of its great values.

The Apostolic Age naturally falls into three periods: 1. The time when the labors of the Apostles were confined to Jerusalem; 2. The time during which their ministrations were performed in all of Palestine; and, 3. The time when they "went into all the world" (the Roman Empire) in obedience to the Savior's behest (Mark 16: 15). The first of these periods includes lessons 1 to 3; the second, lessons 4 to 6; the third, the remaining lessons. It has been thought well to record these three periods in order to show you the rapid growth and expansion of the work. Taking into account the fact that the laborers in the ministry were comparatively few, and the entire time from the endowment of the Apostles to Paul's arrival in Rome was only thirty years, the work of spreading the Gospel made rapid progress. This progress is best illustrated by the rapidity with which the periods follow each other.

There is scarcely a movement, religious or otherwise, in the history of the world, which can be compared, in quickness of development, with the first thirty years of the spread of Christianity. Up to the year 33 A. D., the name of Christ had scarcely been heard outside of a region no greater than one of the larger counties of Utah; over all the civilized world beside, paganism and Judaism held undisputed sway. Yet, by the year 63 A. D., through the active zeal of our Lord's followers, His name and the doctrines He came to establish had spread over Syria, Asia Minor, Arabia, Greece, Italy, and, we donot not, some regions farther west. The Christians, as the followers of Jesus were called in derision first in Antioch, (Acts 11: 26) were everywhere known, and everywhere spoken evil against. Opposed by the combined forces of the two widely accepted religions above mentioned, the Gospel of Christ had spread "to the ends of the earth," and had been accepted by Jews and pagans everywhere.

Progress so rapid seemed to promise great things for the future. But the fact soon became apparent that these promises were not to be fulfilled in that age. The progress of the great work was suddenly checked. Anti-Christ combined all its forces and hurled them against the Truth, now weakened by death, dissension, heresy, and apostacy. This onslaught was successful; and the great things which seemed to be promised in the primitive Church were denied fulfillment. This outcome, so surprising to us at first glance, is found, upon afterthought, to have been a part of God's design. The time was not yet ripe for the final triumph of the Cause of Truth. Therefore, jealousies and dissensions between men prominent in the work, (carefully screened in the Acts, yet painfully apparent in the Epistles), heresies, failure to keep the quorums completely organized, the rise of false teachers—these and other evils were allowed, in the providence of God, to grow and to weaken the Truth in the presence of its enemies, that it might, for the time being, be crushed to earth, to rise in greater completeness and glory, and triumph in our own time.

We wish you to study this great subject in the light of this brief explanation, with the understanding that the world at that time was not ready for the saving power of pure Christianity; but that the work then performed was necessary to assist in the bringing about of the world's present preparation for the Gospel as revealed through the Prophet Joseph Smith.

For suggestions as to the proper method of studying this subject, we refer you to the preceding Manual. It may not be out of place, however, to repeat some of those hints, by way of emphasis. We are especially anxious that you "get at the kernel" of each topic. Some of the notes and some of the lessons are necessarily long, having been made so for the sake of fullness of treatment. Yet to one who reads the *meaning*, rather than the *words* merely, the longest of these will quickly become clear. If you always look for the thought, you will have no difficulty in readily mastering it. Then, if you get into the habit of *reading* the thought, it will be an easy step to the habit of *speaking* it; and we would urge you to cultivate both these habits.

Of course it is expected that one of the lessons shall be treated each evening. If this is carefully looked after, it will be an easy matter for you to complete the course during the season and we are very desirous that all associations shall do this, in order that fragmentary work on the last few lessons may not need to be done during the summer. If too much of each lesson is not assigned to one individual, but if it is divided among a number, and they are careful to make *short, pithy* talks on the topics, you will be much more likely to finish the lesson, in addition to securing greater variety in your meetings, and bringing a larger number of the young men into the work.

Study carefully the map of each country treated, and learn something of its people and their history and condition in the Apostolic age. The notes will help you in this, and you should also make good use of Bible Helps, Concordances, Dictionaries, Encyclopædias, etc. Thus, by brief lectures, pointed discussions, and full treatment of the review questions, you may secure a reasonably full knowledge of each subject. In order to render you further assistance in mastering these details, we have placed in the back of this manual a pronouncing glossary of all the proper names which appear in the lessons. This will help you to form the valuable habit of pronouncing names correctly. It is not enough that you find the location of the various places mentioned; if they are connected with one or more of the missionary journeys detailed in the Acts, the entire journey should be traced, with all the localities visited named in their order. We would suggest that where no wall map like the one presented to you in the Manual, can be had, a suggestive outline map be drawn on the blackboard, or elsewhere, to illustrate each successive event.

As in your study of the Life of Jesus, we desire that you consider the principles of the Gospel as they were presented during the Apostolic age. An advantage will be found in the fact that in several places in the Acts the first principles are presented in their regular order; and the *order* of these principles is next in importance to the doctrines themselves.

In conclusion, permit us to repeat the suggestions presented in the former Manual:

1. Talk directly to the subject. 2. Master all its necessary details. 3. Practice stopping at the right time and place. 4. Do not allow endless, rambling discussion. 5. Avoid the introduction of mysteries. 6. Use your own language, in preference to reading or reciting the words of others. 7. Master the notes as thoroughly as possible. 8. Use correct language. 9. Practice ease and grace in speaking. 10. Cultivate the habit of correctly quoting important passages of scripture. 11. Study the philosophy of events. 12. Testimony bearing may occasionally be allowed by way of increasing faith. 13. Prepare all lessons thoroughly, whether appointed to treat them or not. 14. Make ample and careful use of the map. 15. Get the Spirit of God and *work hard* under its direction.

With earnest solicitude for your advancement, and ever praying for your continued and increased success, we remain,

Your brethren and co-workers,

THE COMMITTEE.

# THE APOSTOLIC AGE.

## PERIOD I.

### MINISTRY IN JERUSALEM AND VICINITY.

#### LESSON I.

#### ENDOWMENT OF THE APOSTLES.

| EVENTS. (A. D. 33.) | REFERENCES.* |
|---|---|
| 1. **The Ascension of Christ.** *Note 1.* | |
|   *a.* The Apostles are taught pertaining to the Kingdom of God. | Acts 1: 3. |
|   *b.* Commanded to tarry in Jerusalem and the Holy Ghost promised. | Acts 1: 4-5. |
|   *c.* Their question concerning the restoration of the kingdom to Israel and the Savior's reply. | Acts 1: 6-8. |
|   *d.* The Ascension, the appearance of the angel and his prophecy concerning the second coming of the Lord. | Acts 1: 9-11. |
| 2. **The Quorum of the Apostles Filled.** | |
|   *a.* The meetings at the abode of the Apostles—Their names. | Acts 1: 12-14. |

\*—The student is referred to "Roberts' Outlines of Ecclesiastical History," Part I, Section VII, and to the "New Witness for God," by the same author, Chapter VIII, for interesting matter relating to this lesson.

|   |   |   |
|---|---|---|
| *b.* | Peter's discourse to the disciples. *Note 2.* | Acts 1: 15-22. |
| *c.* | The disciples seek the inspiration of the Lord. | Acts 1: 23-25. |
| *d.* | Matthias chosen. *Note 3.* | Acts 1: 26. |

3. **The Holy Ghost Manifested.**
    *a.* The meeting on the day of Pentecost. *Note 4.* — Acts 2: 1.
    *b.* The rushing wind—the cloven tongues of fire—filled with the Holy Ghost. — Acts 2: 2-4.
    *c.* Devout Jews confounded by the gift of tongues. — Acts 2: 5-12.
    *d.* Mockers accuse the disciples of drunkenness. — Acts 2: 13.

4. **The First Gospel Sermon.**
    *a.* Peter defends the disciples and refers to the prophecy of Joel. *Note 5.* — Acts 2: 14-21.
    *b.* He tells the people that they have crucified the Christ, the Lord. — Acts 2: 22-36.
    *c.* The question of the repentant Jews—"What shall we do?" — Acts 2: 37.
    *d.* Peter's reply—He proclaims the first principles of the Gospel. *Note 6.* — Acts 2: 38-40.

5. **First Additions to the Church.**
    *a.* Three thousand added to the church by baptism. — Acts 2: 41.
    *b.* The gifts of the Spirit exercised by the Apostles. — Acts 2: 42-43.
    *c.* Daily additions to the church. — Acts 2:47.

## NOTES.

1. The Acts of the Apostles is described as a second treatise by St. Luke, and it commences with the inscription to the same Theophilus whom the evangelist addresses in his gospel. It is a continuation of the life of our Lord, who through the promised Spirit is manifested on earth in the

deeds and preaching of the Apostles. Hence it has been called the Gospel of the Spirit. The time and place of writing are left to be gathered from indirect notices. But it is most probable that St. Luke wrote it at Rome, whither he accompanied St. Paul (Acts 28.). The fact that he mentions events of contemporary history as one living amongst them, and nowhere alludes to the fall of Jerusalem, makes it certain that it was written before that event; and as the narrative terminates about the year A. D. 61, its composition must have been soon after that date, and probably not later than A. D. 63. The book is a Book of Origins. It is the earliest sketch of the foundation and spread of the Christian Church. It tells of the first Apostolic miracle, the first Apostolic sermon, the rise of ecclesiastical organization, the first persecution, the first martyr, the first Gentile convert, and the first European church. Thus we trace the progress of the Christian Society from a small Jewish sect to a universal Church. The same marks of Catholicity as regards the offer of the Glad Tidings to the entire human race, which we notice in the third Gospel, are maintained in the Acts; only what is in the Gospel prophecy, indication, type, and parable, is in the Acts (largely) converted into fulfillment, fact, and history; and though the book touches in all directions upon contemporary events, politics, topography, yet "no ancient work," to use the words of Bishop Lightfoot, "affords at so many points, so many tests of veracity." (Oxford Bible Helps.)

2. The selection of an Apostle to fill the vacancy caused by the death of Judas is conclusive evidence that the organization of the church as the Apostles (fresh from the personal teaching and instruction of the Master, see Acts 1: 3), understood it, included among its permanent features *Twelve Apostles;* and that the perpetuation of the *quorum* of the Twelve Apostles was a part of the original plan and order of the organization of the Church of Christ; and only the gradual departure from that original plan, and final complete apostacy, prevented the perfect organization from being perpetuated.

3. In consequence of Matthias having been chosen by "lot" it may be a question in the minds of some as to his being called of God. A careful consideration of all that was done in connection with the circumstance will dispel all doubt in relation to it. It must be observed that after Joseph Barsabas and Matthias were nominated for the place in the quorum of the Twelve, the Apostles prayed, saying: "Thou Lord, which knowest the hearts of all men, show whether of these two *Thou* hast chosen." Before his ascension Jesus had said to these men: "If ye abide in me, and my words abide in you, ye shall ask what ye will, and it shall be done unto you. * * * Ye have not chosen me, but I have chosen you, and ordained you; * * * that whatsoever ye shall ask of the Father in my name, he may give it you." Therefore when the Apostles asked which of the two men nominated God had chosen and they gave their votes and Matthias was the one selected: God in that way answered their prayer and Matthias was thus called of God. Again, to be called by a divinely appointed

authority is to be called of God. No one can deny that the Apostles were a divinely appointed authority, hence, to be called by them was to be called of God. (Roberts' Outlines of Ecclesiastical History, Note 1, Page 83.)

4. The Day of Pentecost, from the Greek word for the fiftieth day, was the day on which was kept the Feast of Weeks or of Harvest, at the end of seven complete weeks from the 16th of Nisan. The passages bearing on it will be found in Exodus 23; 16; Lev. 23: 15-21; Num. 28: 26-31. The festival lasted but one day. Its chief feature was the offering of two leavened loaves made from the new corn of the now completed harvest, which together with two lambs as a thank offering were waved before the Lord. It was preeminently an expression of gratitude for the harvest, which began with the first ripe sheaf of barley at the passover and ended with that of the two loaves of the newly ripened wheat. In its festive joy the servants and strangers, the fatherless and the widow, were to share with the freeborn Israelites. (Deut. 6, 11.) (Oxford Bible Helps.) See also Roberts' Outlines of Ecclesiastical History, footnote page 74 and note 2, page 83.

5. It is very generally supposed among Christians that this outpouring of the Holy Ghost on the day of Pentecost was the fulfillment of Joel's prophecy, that is, its complete fulfillment. A careful examination of the prophecy, however, will clearly demonstrate that this is not the case. The prophecy will be found in Joel 2: 28-32, and the particulars enumerated in it are as follows: The spirit of the Lord is to be poured out upon *all flesh*: at Pentecost it was poured out upon a few of the disciples of Jesus only. The sons and daughters of the people were to prophesy; we have no account of their doing so at Pentecost. Old men were to dream dreams and young men see visions; there is no account of this taking place on the occasion in question. Wonders were to be shown in the heavens and in the earth, blood and fire and pillars of smoke, the sun was to be turned into darkness, the moon into blood, before the great and terrible day of the Lord come, yet on Mount Zion and in Jerusalem deliverance was to be found. These things unquestionably point to the glorious coming of the Son of God to judgment (See Matt. 24); and certainly they were not fulfilled on the day of Pentecost by the outpouring of the Holy Ghost on a few of the disciples of Jesus. Still Peter said, referring to the spirit poured out upon the disciples, "This is that which was spoken by the prophet Joel," and then quoted the passage. He doubtless meant: This spirit which you now see poured out upon these few men is that spirit which Joel spoke of, and which will eventually be poured out upon *all flesh*, not only upon men and women, but upon the brute creation as well, so that the lion and lamb shall lie down together and a little child shall lead them, and they shall not hurt nor destroy in all God's holy mountain. I have deemed it necessary to make this note, first, because of the very general belief among Christians that the prophecy of Joel was fulfilled on the day of Pentecost; and, second, because the prophecy is one that was quoted by the angel Moroni on the occasion of his first visit to Joseph Smith, con-

cerning which he said it was not yet fulfilled but soon would be (Pearl of Great Price, page 50); hence, since this heavenly messenger puts its fulfillment in the future, it could not have been fulfilled on the day of Pentecost, two thousand years ago. (Roberts' Outlines of Ecclesiastical History, Note 3, page 83. See also Roberts' "New Witness for God," pages 147-149).

6. It will be seen that in this sermon the Apostle Peter presented the principles of the Gospel in the same order as John the Baptist and the Savior had presented them, namely, Faith in God, Repentance of sin, Baptism by immersion for the remission of sin, and the promise of the Holy Ghost.

## REVIEW.

1. Of what is the book called the "Acts of the Apostles" a record? 2. By whom is it believed to have been written? 3. What evidence is there that it was written by Luke? 4. What did Jesus teach the apostles after his resurrection and before his ascension? 5. What command did he give them? 6. What did the angel say to the apostles concerning the second coming of Jesus? 7. Where did the apostles go after witnessing the ascension of the Lord? 8. What were the names of the eleven apostles? 9. To what business did the apostles attend soon after the ascension of the Savior? 10. In his discourse to the disciples at this time what did Peter say concerning Judas? 11. What concerning the necessity of choosing an apostle? 12. Who were nominated for the vacancy? 13. Who was chosen? 14. In what manner was he chosen? 15. Was Matthias called of God? Give reasons. 16. What Jewish feast was kept on the Day of Pentecost? 17. What great blessing was bestowed upon the Saints on the Day of Pentecost? 18. How was the Holy Ghost manifested on this occasion? 19. What did Peter say to the mockers in relation to this outpouring of the Holy Ghost? 20. What erroneous belief is held by the Christian world concerning the fulfillment of the prophecy of Joel on the Day of Pentecost? 21. What is the correct explanation of Peter's reference to Joel's prophecy? 22. What dreadful thing did Peter tell the Jews they had done? 23. What effect did Peter's discourse have upon his hearers? 24. What important question did they ask? 25. What was Peter's reply? 26. What principles of the Gospel were presented by Peter in this sermon and in what order? 27. What act was performed by those who "gladly received Peter's word?" 28. How many were added to the church that day?

## LESSON II.

## THE WORK IN JERUSALEM.

|     | EVENTS. (A. D. 33.) | REFERENCES. |
| --- | --- | --- |
| 1.  | **The Cripple Healed.** | |
| a.  | The lame man at the Beautiful gate, healed in the name of Jesus. | Acts 3: 1-7. |
| b.  | He praises God. | Acts 3: 8-10. |
| 2.  | **Peter's Address.** | |
| a.  | He preaches Christ to those who crucified him. *Note 1.* | Acts 3: 11-26. |
| 3.  | **First Examination Before the Priests.** | |
| a.  | Peter and John arrested and imprisoned. | Acts 4: 1-3. |
| b.  | The authority of the Apostles questioned. | Acts 4: 5-7. |
| c.  | Peter's answer. | Acts 4: 8-12. |
| d.  | Peter and John forbidden by the priests to teach in the name of Jesus. | Acts 4: 13-18. |
| e.  | Peter's answer. | Acts 4: 19-20. |
| f.  | They report to "their own company." | Acts 4: 21-23. |
| g.  | The effect of the report. *Note 2.* | Acts 4: 24-31. |
| 4.  | **"All Things Common."** | Acts 4:32-37. Doc & Cov Sec. 51. Roberts' Ecc'l. Hist. part IV, pp. 352-6. |
| a.  | The believers have all things common. | Acts 4: 32. |
| b.  | Possessions sold. | Acts 4: 34-37. |
| 5.  | **Ananias and Sapphira.** | |
| a.  | Their duplicity. | Acts 5: 1-2. |
| b.  | Peter's reproof. | Acts 5: 3-4. |
| c.  | Death of Ananias and Sapphira. | Acts 5: 5-11. |

## NOTES.

1. Peter's exortation to the people who gathered round him after the healing of the lame man is remarkable. Evidently many of them, at least, had taken active part in the crucifixion of Jesus, though Peter believed they had done it ignorantly. (Acts 3: 17.) He therefore holds out to them some hope of eventual, not immediate, pardon when he says (Acts 3. 19 and 20): " Repent ye, therefore, and be converted, that your sins *may* be blotted out, *when the times of refreshing shall come from the presence of the Lord; and he shall send Jesus Christ, which before was preached unto you.*" Note the difference between these words and those addressed to the repentant on the day of Pentecost: "Repent, and be baptized, *every one of you* in the name of Jesus Christ *for the remission of sins* and ye *shall receive the gift of the Holy Ghost.*" (Acts 2: 38.)

2. This is the second recorded outpouring of the Holy Ghost upon the apostles since the ascension of the Savior, and it is wonderful what a change is wrought upon them by this endowment. We are told in the text that "they (all) spake the word of God with *boldness.*" (Chap. 4: 31.) Contrast the timid Peter who declared: "I know not this man of whom ye speak," (Mark 14: 71) with the intrepid apostle who, no longer afraid to own his Lord, with the greatest boldness proclaims Him on all occasions and fearlessly accuses those who crucified Him; and when commanded by the high priests and elders not to speak or teach in the name of Jesus replies without fear: "Whether it be right in the sight of God to hearken unto you more than unto God, judge ye. For we cannot but speak the things which we have seen and heard."

## REVIEW.

1. What miracle did Peter perform as he and John went up to the temple? 2. What did the healed man do? 3. What effect did this miracle have upon the people? 4. What remarkable statement did Peter make to the people who "ran together" unto the apostles? 5. What effect did Peter's sermon have upon the people? (Acts 4: 4.) 6. What upon the Priests? 7. What did they do to Peter and John? 8. What question did they put to them on the morrow? 9. Repeat the reply of Peter. (Chap. 4. verses 8 to 12.) 10. What course did the high priests pursue when they saw the boldness of Peter? 11. What command did they give to Peter and John? 12. What reply did the apostles make? 13. When the two apostles were set free what did they do? 14. What did the company of the disciples do when they heard the report of Peter and John? 15 What did they ask the Lord to grant them? 16. What occurred in answer to their prayer? 17. What effect did these outpourings of the Holy Ghost produce upon the disciples? 18. What course did the saints pursue in relation to their worldly possessions? 19. How did Ananias and Sapphira attempt to deceive the apostles? 20. Quote Peter's rebuke. 21. What was the result of their dishonesty?

## LESSON III.

## THE RISE OF PERSECUTION.

| EVENTS. (A. D. 33.) | REFERENCES. |
|---|---|
| 1. **Public Teachings and Miracles.** | |
|   *a.* The Apostles teach in the temple and work many miracles. *Note 1.* | Acts 5: 12. |
|   *b.* Multitudes added to the church. | Acts 5: 13-14. |
|   *c.* The sick brought into the streets to be healed. *Note 2.* | Acts 5: 15-16. |
| 2. **Persecution by the Sadducees and others.** | |
|   *a.* The high priests' indignation. | Acts 5: 17. |
|   *b.* Arrest and imprisonment. | Acts 5: 18. |
|   *c.* Delivered by an Angel. | Acts 5: 19-20. |
|   *d.* The council called. | Acts 5: 21. |
|   *e.* The second arrest and examination before the priests. | Acts 5: 21-28. |
|   *f.* Peter's answer. | Acts 5: 29-32. |
|   *g.* The evil counsel. | Acts 5: 33. |
|   *h.* Gamaliel. | Acts 5: 34-39. |
|   *i.* The Apostles scourged. | Acts 5: 40-42. |
| 3. **Seven Wise Men Chosen.** | |
|   *a.* Their qualifications — Duties — Names. *Note 3.* | Acts 6: 1-6. |
|   *b.* Stephen's good works. | Acts 6: 8. |
|   *c.* False witness against him — His glorious appearance. | Acts 6: 9-15. |
| 4. **Stephen's Martyrdom.** | |
|   *a.* His defense before the council. | Acts 7: 1-50. |
|   *b.* The priests arraigned. | Acts 7: 51-54. |
|   *c.* Stephen's glorious testimony. | Acts 7: 55-56. |
|   *d.* He is cast out and stoned. | Acts 7: 57-60. |
|   *e.* The young man Saul. | { Acts 7: 58. <br> { Acts 8: 1-2. |

## NOTES.

1. The exercise of Spiritual Gifts is one of the evidences of the true Gospel. Jesus said to his apostles, after commanding them to preach the Gospel to every creature, "And these signs shall follow them that believe; in my name they shall cast out devils; they shall speak with new tongues; they shall take up serpents; and if they drink any deadly thing it shall not hurt them; they shall lay hands on the sick and they shall recover." (Mark 16: 15-18). This was an emphatic statement, "These signs shall follow them that believe," and although, it is true, that the performance of miracles, or what appear to be such, is not always proof of the truth, it is a fact that the true church of Christ will always be accompanied by the "signs" promised by the Savior. The Church of Jesus Christ of Latter-day Saints has been abundantly blessed with the "Gifts of the Spirit" and the saints enjoy them today as these gifts were enjoyed anciently.

2. The account of the wonderful gift of healing enjoyed by the apostles at the time referred to in our lesson, when the sick were brought by the multitude "into the streets and laid on beds and couches, that at the least the shadow of Peter passing by might overshadow some of them," brings to mind the marvelous display of the power of God through the Prophet Joseph Smith and the apostles in this dispensation. On July 22nd, 1839, at Commerce, afterwards called Nauvoo, the saints were lying sick in great numbers, on both sides of the river. The prophet himself was very sick, but being filled with a great desire to attend to the duties of his calling, he rose from his bed, and commencing at his own house, went from house to house and healed all the sick who lay in his path. He crossed the river, taking Elder Heber C. Kimball with him, and healed Elder Brigham Young and many others. While waiting at the ferry, to re-cross the river on his way home, a man who had seen this mighty manifestation of the power of God, asked him to go and heal two of his children who were very sick. The prophet replied that he could not go, but would send some one to heal them. Then calling Elder Wilford Woodruff, he told him to go with the man and heal his children, and giving him a silk handkerchief, told him to wipe the faces of the children with it and they should be healed. Elder Woodruff did as he was directed and the children were healed. President Woodruff still has the handkerchief. Many remarkable cases of healing have occurred and still occur in the church of Christ in this day. A number of such are recorded in Roberts' "New Witness for God," Chapter XVIII, to which the student is referred.

3. The men chosen on this occasion are commonly called the seven deacons, though there seems to be no warrant for so naming them. They are not called deacons anywhere in the Acts nor elsewhere in the New Testament. They appear to have been chosen to meet special circumstances existing at that time in the church at Jerusalem, pertaining to the daily distribution of supplies to the people, who, it will be remembered, "had all things common." That they certainly held priesthood higher than the office of deacon as it is known in the church of Christ today, is proved

by the fact that Philip, who was one of the seven, preached the Gospel to and baptized the Samaritans. (Acts 8: 12), and also baptized the Ethiopian on the way to Jerusalem (Acts 8: 38). Stephen, also, evidently exercised functions higher than those of a deacon in this dispensation (Acts 6: 8). The account given in the text of the choosing of these men is that on account of some murmuring of the Grecians against the Hebrews because of alleged discrimination against the widows of the former, the apostles, not desiring to be taken from their specific duty of teaching the word of God, to attend to temporal affairs, directed the people to choose "seven men of honest report, full of the Holy Ghost and wisdom." Evidently the saints chose such men without regard to their office in the priesthood, and there is no good reason to suppose that there was a special order of priesthood organized or established whose duty it was to attend to this work. They were probably simply a committee of wise and prudent men chosen to relieve the apostles of the burden of these temporal duties.

## REVIEW

1. What effect did the preaching and miracles of the apostles have upon the priests? 2. What did they do? 3. By whom were the apostles delivered from prison? 4. What instructions did the angel give them? 5. What did the priests do when they learned that the apostles were at liberty? 6. What question did they ask of the apostles when they were brought before them? 7. Repeat the apostles' reply. (Acts 5: 29-32). 8. What effect did this reply have on the priests? 9. Who stood up in the council and gave wholesome advice? 10. Who was Gamaliel? 11. What was his advice? (Repeat his words. Acts 5: 35-39). 12. What course did the priests pursue? 13. What complaint was made by the Grecians against the Hebrews in the church? 14. What did the apostles instruct the people to do? 15. What were to be the qualifications of the men chosen? 16. What were to be their duties? 17. Who were chosen? 18. What works did Stephen perform? 19. What course did his enemies pursue to obtain evidence against him? 20. What answer did Stephen make to the accusations brought against him? 21. What effect did Stephen's discourse have upon them? 22. What glorious testimony did Stephen bear? 23. What then did his enemies do to Stephen? 24. What were Stephen's last words? 25. At whose feet did Stephen's murderers lay their clothes?

# LESSON IV.

## EVENTS BEYOND JERUSALEM.

| EVENTS. (A. D. 34.) | REFERENCES. |
|---|---|
| 1. **Philip at Samaria.** *Note 1.* | |
|   *a.* Preaching Christ. | Acts 8: 5-6. |
|   *b.* Miracles Performed. | Acts 8: 7-8. Mark 16: 15-18. |
|   *c.* Conversion of Simon. | Acts 8: 9-13. |
| 2. **Peter and John at Samaria.** | |
|   *a.* Object of the apostles' visit. *Note 2.* | Acts 8: 15-17. |
|   *b.* Simon's misconception of the genius of the Gospel. *Note 3.* | Acts 8: 18-19. |
|   *c.* Peter's rebuke and Simon's repentance. *Note 4.* | Acts 8: 20-24. |
|   *d.* Return of the apostles. | Acts 8: 25. |
| 3. **Philip and the Eunuch.** *Note 5.* | |
|   *a.* Philip guided by inspiration. *Note 6.* | Acts 8: 26-31. Psalms 68: 31. |
|   *b.* The eunuch's scripture reading and questions. | Acts 8: 32-34. Isaiah 53: 7-8. |
|   *c.* Baptized by Philip. | Acts 8: 35-38. |
|   *d.* Philip's disappearance and further labors. *Note 7.* | Acts 8: 39-40. |

## NOTES.

1. The stoning of Stephen seems to have been the culmination of a series of persecutions of the saints in Jerusalem which compelled them to scatter abroad in various parts of Palestine. The apostles and disciples, being filled with enthusiasm and zeal for the spread of the truth, preached the gospel with power wherever they went and thus opened the gospel door to the people beyond Jerusalem. Philip, surnamed "the Evangelist," was the first in this mission. At an early period he was confounded with Philip, the apostle, of whom nothing is known after the election of

Matthias to succeed Judas Iscariot. The statement by biblical scholars that Philip was a deacon only, must not be taken as authority, since from modern revelation it is evident that, baptizing, he must have held a higher priesthood than the office of deacon, probably that of a priest. It should here be observed that the title "Evangelist," applied to Philip, is used in the Church of Jesus Christ of Latter-day Saints to designate a patriarch. In the life of Joseph Smith, under date of June 27, 1839, this is recorded. "An Evangelist is a Patriarch, even the oldest man of the blood of Joseph or of the seed of Abraham." (See also Doctrine and Covenants, 107: 39).

2. While Philip had power to baptize, it would appear that he did not hold that portion of the priesthood which gave him authority to confer the Holy Ghost. On this account, doubtless, the apostles went to Samaria that they might confer the Holy Ghost upon those who had believed the words of Philip; and, having believed, had been baptized, thus complying with the ordinance of the gospel which follows belief and repentance. From this one instance of the bestowal of the Holy Ghost by the apostles, the Catholics have made the erroneous claim that only their Bishops, who profess to be the successors of the apostles, have the authority to confirm members of the church. In the first place, we deny that the Catholic Bishops are the successors of the apostles. Secondly, clear inferences from Acts 15: 39 and 18: 26-28, regarding the ministry of Barnabas, Silas and Apollos. none of whom was an apostle, would lead us to believe that these men must have baptized and confirmed, as there is no doubt that they converted many in their missionary labors. But all question is set at rest by the revelation on that subject recorded in the Doctrine and Covenants, 20: 41-43. where it is distinctly stated that an Elder may perform this ordinance.

3. Simon, surnamed Magus, (the magician), was a sorcerer of Samaria. He was later the founder of a heretical sect, whose doctrines were oriental in form and pretension, among them being the belief in the transmigration of the soul. He assumed all the attributes of the Diety. He had a companion, Helena, whom his enemies designated as a fallen woman. From his doctrines and pretensions and from his later acts, Peter evidently read him aright when he said unto him: "I perceive that thou art in the gall of bitterness and in the bond of iniquity." It is stated, although the tradition has not been confirmed, that Simon subsequently went to Rome, and practicing his arts there, came again in contact with Peter. The legend is that (quoting Farrar), "the imposter, after failing to raise a dead youth—a miracle which St. Peter accomplished—finally attempted to delude the people by asserting that he would fly to heaven; but, at the prayer of St. Peter and St. Paul, he was deserted by the demons who supported him, and dashed bleeding to the earth."

4. That signs were to follow the believers and were not necessarily instituted for converting unbelievers, may be gathered from this incident in Samaria. In the case of Simon, however, it appears that his professed conversion resulted because of the miracles, through which he hoped to

gain pecuniary benefit, and not because of the faith and repentance that must precede baptism, in case the convert truly becomes a member of Christ's church. The rebuke which Peter administered to him should be a strong lesson illustrating the necessity of thorough repentance in order that the remission of sins through baptism may prove effectual.

5. The eunuch here referred to is not named, but was evidently a man of great authority, being the high treasurer, under Candace a hereditary title of the queens of Meroe, in upper Nubia, Africa, like the name of *Pharaoh* applied to the older Egyptian kings.

6. Some may wonder why the Lord should call directly upon Philip to perform this special mission. Why should he not be directed by the apostles, who were the representatives of the Lord upon the earth? It is sufficient reply to state that while he may have been called by the apostles for this work in a general way, the special calls by the Lord were such as pertained to his labors in the line of his calling, and which every missionary, or even member of the church is entitled to. Striking incidents of this guidance by the spirit, have occurred in the church; some of the most important being recorded in President Woodruff's "Leaves From My Journal," chapters 23, 24, 26, and 27.

7. Observe how strictly Philip followed the order of the Gospel as enunciated by the Savior and as declared by Peter on the Day of Pentecost, (Acts 2: 38), both in preaching collectively to the Samaritans, and individually to the eunuch: First, faith in Jesus Christ; second, repentance, or the casting away of sin; third, the administration of the ordinance of baptism for the remission of past sins; fourth, to be followed by the reception of the Holy Ghost through the laying on of hands by those having authority. Notice also how closely this order resembles the order of the Gospel as taught and practiced by the Latter-day Saints. In this connection a lesson is to be learned regarding the mode of baptism. The statement that Philip and his convert "went down into the water" leaves no doubt that immersion was the form employed in this case. This is also evident from all similar incidents related in the New Testament, as well as from the writings of the early church fathers, all of whom refer to immersion as a matter of course. In the writings of Paul such expressions occur as the following: "buried with him by baptism," (Rom. 6: 4), "buried with him in baptism," (Col. 2:12), "planted together in the likeness of his death," (Rom. 6: 5). For further information see "Ready References," pp. 41, 42.

## REVIEW.

1. What followed the martyrdom of Stephen?  2. Who was Philip? 3. What were the results of his labors at Samaria?  4, What authority did Philip hold?  5. What was the purpose of the visit of Peter and John to Samaria?  6. What was the vocation of Simon Magus?  7. Describe his acceptance of the Gospel.  8. What were the motives which actuated him in his professed conversion?  9. What are the purposes of signs?  10. Quote Peter's rebuke to Simon.  11. Describe as near as can be the route taken

by Philip and the eunuch. 12. What was this officer? 13. Quote the prophesy of Isaiah as read by him. 14. Quote it as it appears in Isaiah. 15. Name the condition upon which this man could be baptized. 16. What would you infer from this lesson to be the correct mode of baptism? 17. What was the order of the first principles of the Gospel as promulgated by Philip? 18. What erroneous ideas did Simon evidently entertain concerning the Gospel?

# LESSON V.

## THE GOSPEL TAKEN TO THE GENTILES.

EVENTS. (A. D. 38-41.) REFERENCES.

1. **Peter's Missionary Tour.**
   - *a.* Healing of Æneas at Lydda. Acts 9: 32-35.
     *Note 1.*
   - *b.* Raising of Tabitha from the dead at Joppa. *Note 2.* Acts 9: 35-43.
2. **Cornelius.**
   - *a.* Character of Cornelius. Acts 10: 1-2.
   - *b.* The Vision of Cornelius. Acts 10: 3-8.
3. **Peter's Vision.**
   - *a.* Its nature. Acts 10: 9-16.
   - *b.* Its purposes. *Note 3.* Acts 10: 28-34.
4. **Peter and Cornelius at Cæsarea.** *Note 4.*
   - *a.* Meeting of Peter and Cornelius. Acts 10: 24-29.
   - *b.* The object of Peter's visit to Cornelius. Acts 10: 30-33.
   - *c.* Peter's gospel sermon. Acts 10: 34-43.
   - *d.* Its immediate results. *Note 5.* Acts 10: 44-48.

## NOTES.

1. Lydda, meaning strife, mentioned as Lod in the Old Testament, is located nine miles southeast of Joppa and twenty-four miles northwest of Jerusalem, on the direct road between these two cities. The water course outside of the town is said still to bear the name of Abi-Butrush (Peter), in memory of the apostle. This city is celebrated as the traditional birth and burial place of St. George.

2. Joppa, now known as Yafa or Jaffa, meaning beauty, is a noted Palestine sea port on the Mediterranean, thirty-three miles northwest of Jerusalem, and is frequently named in biblical history. During the building of Solomon's temple, the cedars of Lebanon were floated down from Tyre to Joppa, whence they were transported by land to Jerusalem. The town was frequently taken and retaken during the wars of the Crusades.

It was stormed by Napoleon in 1799; taken by Mahemet Ali in 1832 and retaken by the Turks in 1840, under whose dominion it now remains. It has a population of 23,000 and is the terminus of the recently completed Jaffa-Jerusalem railway. It has grown since 1870 from a population of 12,000.

3. During the life of Christ the Gospel had been preached mainly to the Jews. After His resurrection He commanded His disciples to preach the Gospel to all nations. Since His ascension, up to this time, it had been preached only to the lost children of the House of Israel, but the time had now come when it should be taken to the Gentiles. To Peter was given the special mission of its introduction to them, and his labors were to be followed by Paul, the specially called apostle to the Gentiles. Peter himself partook of the feeling that existed among the Jews that association with the Gentiles was degrading and polluting. This vision was necessary to convince him that God was no respecter of persons, and that the Savior's injunction: "Go ye therefore, and teach all nations," was to be literally interpreted. Three times he was told that what God had cleansed he had no right to call unclean. The strength of his Jewish antipathy to association with the Gentiles is shown by the fact that notwithstanding the vision he had beheld, it was not until Cornelius had related the visitation of an angel to him, that Peter acknowledged that God was no respecter of persons; even after all this, it seems that the manifestation of the Holy Ghost falling upon the Gentiles was necessary to convince Peter that they were entitled to baptism.

4. Cæsarea in ancient geography was a Mediterranean seaport of Palestine, now Kaisariyeh, situated on the line of the great road from Tyre to Egypt, between Jaffa and Dora, thirty-seven miles north of the former city. It was built by Herod I, in the first decennium before Christ and named in honor of Augustus. It became the residence of the Roman governors in Palestine and was mostly inhabited by a foreign population hostile to the Jews. In A. D. 65 an insurrection arose based upon a dispute between the Jews and the Syrians, regarding the ownership of the city. It ended in a massacre of the Jews, 20,000 being slain in one hour in this city alone. Origen taught a Christian school here, in A. D. 200, and it was the birth place of the church historian Eusebius, who died in A. D. 340. The modern Kaisariyeh is a desolate place of ruins, inhabited only by a few fishermen.

5. Here again, we have an example of the order of the Gospel as preached by the apostles, after the ascension of Christ, set forth as plainly as in the instances mentioned in the previous lesson, the only exception in the order, being that the Holy Ghost descended before baptism on those who heard the Gospel. The reason for this exception, it seems plain, was to impress Peter that these Gentile people, whom his prejudices had taught him to consider unworthy, were entitled to receive the ordinances of the Gospel. So strong was this testimony that Peter was obliged to exclaim: "Can any man forbid water, that these should not be baptized, which have

received the Holy Ghost as well as we?" This reception of the Holy Ghost, however, was only a manifestation of the power of God as a convincing testimony to all present on this particular occasion. That it did in no way exclude, or take the place of, the fourth ordinance of the Gospel is clearly evident. The Prophet Joseph Smith, in a sermon delivered in the grove west of the Nauvoo temple, Sunday, March 20, 1842, said: "There are certain keys, words, and signs belonging to the priesthood which must be observed to obtain the blessing. The sign of Peter was to repent and be baptized for the remission of sins, with the promise of the gift of the Holy Ghost; and in no other way was the gift of the Holy Ghost obtained. There is a difference between the Holy Ghost and the gift of the Holy Ghost. Cornelius received the Holy Ghost before he was baptized, which was the convincing power of God unto him of the truth of the Gospel, but he could not receive the gift of the Holy Ghost until after he was baptized. Had he not taken this sign or ordinance upon him, the Holy Ghost which convinced him of the truth of God would have left him. Until he obeyed these ordinances and received the gift of the Holy Ghost by the laying on of hands, according to the order of God, he could not have healed the sick or commanded an evil spirit to come out of a man, and it obey him; * * * I know that all men will be damned if they do not come in the way which he hath opened and this is the way marked out by the Lord."

## REVIEW.

1. What can you say of Lydda and its situation? 2. What do you know of Joppa? 3. Name and describe the miracles performed by Peter on this mission. 4. What was the character of Cornelius? 5. Show by the vision of Cornelius that belief alone is not sufficient to the obtaining of eternal life. 6. Describe Cæsarea. 7. What did Peter say to Cornelius on his arrival? 8. Give Cornelius' reply. 9. Name the main points in Peter's sermon. 10. Why was the Holy Ghost given before baptism? 11. Give the views of the Prophet Joseph Smith upon this subject.

# LESSON VI.

## PERSECUTION AT JERUSALEM.

| EVENTS. (A. D. 41-44.) | REFERENCES. |
|---|---|
| 1. Peter's Defense of his Ministry to the Gentiles. *Note 1* | Acts 11: 1-18. |
| 2. Cruelty of Herod. (Death of James.) *Note 2.* | Acts 12: 1-3. |
| 3. Imprisonment and Release of Peter. | |
|   *a.* Apprehension of Peter. | Acts 12: 4-5. |
|   *b.* His Release from Prison. | Acts 12: 6-11. |
|   *c.* His appearance at the house of Mary. | Acts 12: 12-17. |
|   *d.* Punishment of the jailers. | Acts 12: 18-19. |
| 4. Miserable Death of Herod. | Acts 12: 20-24. |

## NOTES.

1. It would seem from the Epistle of Paul to the Galatians that, under the Mosaic law, any man who could observe the forms by strict obedience to the mere letter of the law, regardless of the intent of the heart, was justified; and that in the early days of the apostles much of their labor among the new converts was to show them the difference between a life based on such rules and the life lived by the principles of faith and repentance, wherein the motives and intents of the heart would be the plummet by which our acts were to be measured. The Jewish converts, who had formerly been circumcised, did not recognize that in the establishment of the Gospel of Jesus Christ the Mosaic law was fulfilled, including the rite of circumcision. Hence their dispute with Peter on his return to Jerusalem. Some fifteen years later the people of Galatia, who had accepted the gospel under Paul's administration, still held to this belief. This made Paul's epistle necessary. In it he charges that they have been bewitched and declares that they have turned "again to the beggarly elements whereunto ye desire again to be in bondage," the beggarly elements in this case doubtless meaning the Mosaic law, including circumcision. To make it still plainer that the purity of their motives and not the compliance with obsolete

forms, was the true standard of the followers of Christ, he says: "Every man that is circumcised is a debtor to the whole law. * * * * For in Jesus Christ neither circumcision availeth anything, nor uncircumcision; but faith which worketh by love. * * * * For all the law is fulfilled in one word, even in this. Thou shalt love thy neighbor as thyself. * * * * For in Christ Jesus neither circumcision availeth anything, nor uncircumcision, but a new creature." (Gal. 5: 3, 6, 14; 6: 15.)

2. Herod Agrippa I—There were three Herods who have ruled in Palestine up to this time, namely: 1—Herod the Great, the son of Antipater, who died a miserable death shortly after the birth of the Savior. It was he who ordered the slaughter of the children under two years of age in and about Bethlehem. 2—Herod Antipas, a son of Herod the Great, who imprisoned and beheaded John the Baptist, and who sent the Savior to Pilate. 3—Herod Agrippa I, son of Aristobulus, grandson of Herod the Great, and a nephew of Herod Antipas, who instituted the persecution of the Christians at Jerusalem at this time. He ruled by permission of Emperor Claudius over the whole of Palestine with the title of king. To ingratiate himself with the Jews, he offered many sacrifices and conformed to the Mosaic ritual. It was to conciliate the Jews further that he instituted the persecutions at Jerusalem which resulted in the death of James the Elder, son of Zebedee, and which would have caused the death of Peter had he not been miraculously delivered by the angel of God. Herod Agrippa I. had not been ruler over Palestine more than three years when death overtook him in the miserable manner related in our lesson, while he was sitting in the judgment seat at Cæsarea and the people were saluting him as a God. With his son, Herod Agrippa II, or the fourth Herod, ended the rule of the Herods, the whole of Palestine then being taken possession of as Roman territory, and its administration being given over to a procurator under the direction of the governor of Syria. This Herod is known in the New Testament only by the name of Agrippa. It was he before whom Festus brought Paul, and whom Paul almost persuaded to be a Christian (Acts 25, 26.)

## REVIEW.

1. Why was it necessary for Peter to defend his course? 2. What was the result of Peter's defense of his ministry to the Gentiles? 3. What was the belief of the Jews in relation to circumcision? 4. Describe Peter's imprisonment. 5. How was Peter released from prison? 6. Tell of his reception at the house of Mary. 7. State what you can of Herod the Great. 8. Of Herod Antipas. 9. Of Herod Agrippa I. 10. Of Herod Agrippa II. 11. Why did the people of Tyre and Sidon visit King Herod? 12. Why did they desire peace? 13. What was the reply of the people to Herod's oration? 14.—What was the result of Herod's pride and self-esteem?

# PERIOD III.

## MINISTRY TO ALL THE WORLD.

### LESSON VII.

#### PAUL'S CONVERSION AND FIRST MISSIONARY JOURNEY.

| EVENTS. (A. D. 36-44.) | REFERENCES. |
|---|---|
| 1. Conversion of Saul. *Note 1.* | |
|    *a.* On the road to Damascus. | Acts 9: 1-9. |
|    *b.* Saul and Ananias. | Acts 9: 10-19. |
| 2. Sojourn in Damascus and Arabia. | |
|    *a.* At Damascus. | Acts 9: 21-22. |
|    *b.* In Arabia. *Note 2.* | Acts 26: 20.<br>Gal. 1: 15-18. |
| 3. Return to Damascus and Flight to Jerusalem. | Acts 9: 23-25. |
| 4. Visit at Jerusalem. | |
|    *a.* His reception. | Acts 9: 26-29. |
|    *b.* Warned in vision to depart. | Acts 22: 17-21. |
| 5. To Tarsus. *Note 3.* | Acts 9: 29-30. |
| 6. Paul and Barnabas. *Note 4.* | |
|    *a.* Departure of Barnabas from Antioch to Tarsus to seek Saul. | Acts 11: 19-25. |
|    *b.* A year in Antioch. | Acts 11: 25-26. |
|    *c.* Visit to Jerusalem with alms. | Acts 11: 27-30. |

#### PAUL'S FIRST MISSIONARY JOURNEY.

| EVENTS. (A. D. 45.) | REFERENCES. |
|---|---|
| 1. In Antioch in Syria. | |
|    *a.* The call of Paul and Barnabas. *Note 5.* | Acts 13: 1-3. |

2. In Cyprus.
   a. At Salamis — Preaching in the
      Synagogues.                              Acts 13: 4-5.
   b. Events in Paphos.   *Note 6.*            Acts 13: 6-12.
3. To Perga in Pamphylia.
   a. Disagreement with John Mark.            Acts 13: 13.

---

## NOTES.

1. Saul was conscientious, zealous and energetic in all that he undertook, and as a consequence became one of the most bitter of the many persecutors of the early Christians. He was a pupil of Gamaliel who was noted for sound judgment and humane feeling, (See Acts 5: 34-38), but undoubtedly thought that it was a duty to put down what he considered a heresy, that threatened to destroy the system to which all his religious notions were attached. As Paul himself declares, he did it ignorantly, through unbelief. It appears that there had been little hesitation on his part in the havoc he was working up to the time of his journey to Damascus, and upon that he started breathing out threatenings and slaughter, but from the account given of his miraculous conversion, we are justified in concluding that calm reflection was producing trains of thought which greatly disturbed Saul's mind. That at least a partial preparation for the startling events so soon to follow, was going on in his mind is evident from the words of our Savior: "It is hard for thee to kick against the pricks." Very recently Saul had witnessed many wonderful evidences of the divinity of the work he was trying to destroy. He had observed the patient resignation, with which one Christian household after another had borne the cruel persecution, which he himself had heaped upon them. He had listened to the inspired testimony of Stephen, and had gazed into his glorified face and heard his announcement of the radiant vision opened to his sight while his body was being bruised and maimed by stones, while Paul held the raiment of those who perpetrated that cruel murder. Such scenes could not but produce powerful impressions on a mind like Saul's, regardless of his zeal for the cause which he defended. The journey to Damascus, a distance of about 160 miles, over a burning desert with nothing to detract the mind from its own workings, for a period of five or six days, was especially calculated to bring to Saul doubts regarding the course he was pursuing. There are three separate accounts in the Acts of Saul's conversion, (Acts 9: 1-9, Acts 22: 5-11 and Acts 26: 12-20), and that slight variations exist in these accounts is evident to the careful reader. From the fact that Luke writes all three accounts, it is evident that there is design in the variety. The first is a simple historical account of the conversion, while the two latter ones are taken from Paul's addresses, one before the Jewish mob in the Temple court and the other before Festus and Agrippa at Cæsarea. The difference in the audiences to which Paul

was speaking accounts for the difference in the details of the narrative. What would carry weight with the Romans would have only served to hasten the resentment of the Jews.

2. Paul's visit to Arabia. The time and length of Paul's visit to Arabia are somewhat uncertain. Luke in Acts 9: 20, says, Paul *straightway* preached in the synagogues of Damascus, while Paul himself (Gal. 1: 16), says, he *immediately* went into Arabia. It is probable that as a new convert, Paul felt an irresistible impulse to declare the new truths revealed to him and preached for a short time before he retired. Regarding the length of his retirement little is definitely known. From the records we learn that three years intervened between his conversion and his final flight from Damascus. We suppose that fully one year of this time was spent somewhere in the desert solitudes of Arabia, where Paul underwent a spiritual preparation for his great work, and quietly thought out the meaning of that deluge of truth which had suddenly burst into his life.

3. Paul's brief visit of fifteen days at Jerusalem evidently occurred in 39 A. D. Paul left Tarsus for Antioch with Barnabas about 44 A. D., making his stay in the region of Tarsus cover a period of four or five years. Very little is known of what transpired during this time. In Acts 15: 41 Paul is mentioned as going through Syria and Cilicia, confirming the churches, and as no account is given in Acts of the establishment of these churches, good authorities assume that Paul planted them during this period. In Gal. 1: 21-24. Paul speaks of preaching the faith which once he destroyed, as if it was in this region.

4. Barnabas seems to have been impressed with the greatness of Paul's character from the first meeting. When, during his first visit to Jerusalem, the disciples were about to reject his overtures to join himself to them, Barnabas championed his cause before the apostles, and now when sent to Antioch to help in the work of more firmly establishing the churches, he sought the first opportunity of going to Tarsus and seeking out Saul as a companion in the work.

5. This passage forms conclusive proof that the early Christians were taught the necessity of men being called of God, as was Aaron, to preach the Gospel and administer in the ordinances thereof. Nor was it enough for them to be called, but the hands of those in authority were laid upon them and they were set apart for the mission they were about to undertake.

6. In this passage we first observe that the name Saul is changed to Paul. Some suppose that the latter name was assumed out of respect to Sergius Paulus, his distinguished convert, but the conclusion does not seem to be warranted. It was a common custom among the Jews to have two names, one strictly Jewish and the other foreign. The Silas of the Acts is Silvanus in the Epistles, the latter being the Gentile or foreign name. Being born and raised in the city of Tarsus, Paul may always have borne both names, and assumed now the latter because he was going among a foreign people.

## REVIEW.

1 Where was Saul born? 2. To what sect did he belong? 3. What advantages of education did he enjoy? 4. Who was Gamaliel? 5. What part did Saul take in the death of Stephen? 6. What was Saul's purpose in going to Damascus? 7. What evidence have we that Saul's mind was disturbed by the course he was pursuing? 8. How do you explain the differences in the three accounts of Saul's conversion? 9. What special work did the Lord say awaited Saul? 10. What was Saul's purpose in going into Arabia? 11. How was Saul received on his first visit to Jerusalem? 12. About what time elapsed between the conversion of Saul and his entry upon his active ministry? 13. How and where was this time spent? 14. What reasons are there for the opinion that Saul labored as a missionary in the vicinity of Tarsus, during his stay there? 15. On what former occasion did Saul and Barnabas meet, previous to their meeting at Tarsus? 16. Quote the passage containing the call of Saul and Barnabas. 17. What is a synagogue? 18. How do you explain Saul's change of name?

# LESSON VIII.

## PAUL'S FIRST MISSIONARY JOURNEY. (Concluded).

## FIRST CHURCH COUNCIL IN JERUSALEM.

| EVENTS. (A. D. 45-49.) | REFERENCES. |
|---|---|
| 1. At Antioch in Pisidia. | |
|    *a.* Paul's address. | Acts 13: 14-41. |
|    *b.* Rejected by the Jews, they turn to the Gentiles. *Note 1*. | Acts 13: 42-49. |
|    *c.* Departure from Antioch because of persecution. | Acts 13: 50-51. |
| 2. In Iconium. | Acts 14: 1-6. |
| 3. In Lystra. | Acts 14: 6-7. |
|    *a.* Paul heals a lame man. | Acts 14: 8-10. |
|    *b.* An attempt to deify Paul and Barnabas. | Acts 14: 10-18. |
|    *c.* Paul is stoned. *Note 2*. | Acts 14: 19-20. |
| 4. From Derbe to Antioch. *Note 3*. | Acts 14: 20-25. |

## FIRST CHURCH COUNCIL IN JERUSALEM.

| EVENTS. (A. D. 50.) | REFERENCES. |
|---|---|
| 1. Controversy Over Circumcision. | Acts 15: 1. |
| 2. Paul, Barnabas and Titus sent to Jerusalem. *Note 4*. | Acts 15: 2-3.<br>Gal. 2: 1-2. |
| 3. The Meeting at Jerusalem. | |
|    *a.* The question discussed. *Note 5*. | Acts 15: 4-11. |
|    *b.* The formal decision sent to the churches. *Note 6*. | Acts 15: 12-29. |

## NOTES.

1. Though Paul had previously converted the Roman Sergius Paulus and perhaps at other times, during his sojourn in the region of Tarsus, had had occasion to address Gentiles, this appears to be the first time that he discoursed for their especial benefit. He seems not to have lost sight of

the fact that his mission was to them. At his conversion, the Lord indicated to him his special calling and again in the vision in the Temple, in which he was warned to flee from Jerusalem, he was told that he would be sent far hence unto the Gentiles (Acts 22: 21).

2. At the time of his conversion the Lord said he would show Paul how great things he must suffer for His name's sake (Acts 9: 16), and during his career this promise was faithfully kept. Paul suffered many times over all the cruelties he had heaped upon the Christians. As the infuriated mob rushed on him with stones here at Lystra, the death of Stephen and the part he took in it, must have come again fresh to his mind and caused him suffering as keen as the bodily wounds he received. Though driven from Lystra by the bitterest of persecution, his labors were not without rich fruit. It was here that the beloved Timothy, his future friend and companion, together with his mother Eunice and his grandmother Lois, was converted.

3. The time occupied in this missionary journey cannot be determined with any certainty. The time of departure is quite definitely placed in the year 45 A. D. The council at Jerusalem, which Paul and Barnabas visited some time after their return, at which their labors were reported, was held in the year 50 A. D., so that the entire time between these two events, their departure and their visit to Jerusalem, must have covered between four and five years. We are told that they abode at Antioch after their return, no little time. It seems safe to say that their mission did not occupy more than two or two and a half years.

4. Though Jesus had plainly announced that while He came not to destroy the law, He did come to fulfill it, there were many who could not readily understand that the old ritual, much of which was merely a symbol of His great sacrifice, had been done away in the new covenant into which they had entered, hence this controversy over circumcision. In addition to the convincing testimonies of Paul and Barnabas, as to what the Lord had done for the Gentiles without circumcision, Titus, a Greek, was there as an evidence of the fruits of the Gospel among the Gentiles. From Gal. 2: 2, it appears that Paul was obeying the voice of revelation in undertaking his mission to Jerusalem.

5. The remarks of James. From the fact that James presided at this council, the idea has been held by some, that he might have been the head of the church at this time. From Acts 15: 19, it is evident that he rendered the decision of the council in this case, but this may be explained by the fact that Peter was an interested party in the controversy, since he had admitted the Gentile Cornelius to membership without circumcision, and doubtless preferred not to sit in judgment on a case where his own actions had committed him to a certain course; hence, James was called upon to preside.

6. Special attention should be given to verse 28, which reads: "For it seemed good *to the Holy Ghost* and to us, to lay upon you no greater burden than these necessary things." From this statement it is evident

that the members of the council depended upon, and were guided by the Holy Ghost in their deliberations and decisions. This is important as showing that the ancient church, in its early history, was presided over by a united body of inspired men, possessing the Priesthood of presidency, and kept in the path of wisdom by inspiration and revelation. If the unity of the church had been preserved by this presiding body being perpetuated, there probably would not have been a great apostacy a century after this time. Therein is the safeguard of the church today, in keeping the quorums intact, and in the continued revelation to them of the mind and will of God concerning their duties.

## REVIEW.

1. Over what kind of country would the journey from Perga to Antioch, in Pisidia, lead the missionaries? 2. What part of the country was occupied by the Galatians? 3. What prediction was partially fulfilled by the persecutions Paul suffered on this journey? 4. At what point of the journey did they commence their formal mission to the Gentiles? 5. What persons are named as being converted on this journey? 6. What mountains separated Paul from his old home when he reached Derbe? 7. What time was occupied in this mission? 8. When was the Council of Jerusalem held? 9. For what purpose was it called? 10. Who accompanied Paul on this journey? 11. What argument did Peter make on the question under discussion? 12. How was the question finally disposed of? 13. How do you account for the fact that James presided and passed judgment on the question? 14. Show the importance of organization and inspiration in preserving the unity of the church.

# LESSON IX.

## PAUL'S SECOND MISSIONARY JOURNEY.

| EVENTS. (A. D. 53-55). | REFERENCES. |
|---|---|

1. **Separation of Paul and Barnabas.**
   *Note 1.*
   a. Barnabas takes Mark and goes to Cyprus.   Acts 15: 36-39.
   b. Paul chooses Cyrus and goes through Syria and Cilicia. *Note 2.*   Acts 15: 40-41.
2. **Timothy Accompanies Paul From Lystra.** *Note 3.*   Acts 16: 1-5.
3. **Through Phrygia and Galatia.** *Note 4.*   Acts 16: 6.
4. **In Troas.**
   a. Paul's Vision.   Acts 16: 7-9.
   b. Joined by Luke. *Note 5.*   Acts 16: 10-11.
5. **In Philippi.**
   a. The conversion of Lydia.   Acts 16: 13-15.
   b. Healing of the demoniac girl.   Acts 16: 16-18.
   c. Paul and Silas imprisoned.   Acts 16: 19-24.
   d. The earthquake and conversion of the jailer.   Acts 16: 25-34.
   e. Release and departure from Philippi.   Acts 16: 35-40.
6. **In Thessalonica.**
   a. Discourse in the synagogue.   Acts 17: 1-4.
   b. Jason before the magistrate.   Acts 17: 5-9.
7. **In Berea.**
   a. Preaching in the synagogue.   Acts 17: 10-12.
   b. Opposition of Jews from Thessalonica.   Acts 17: 13.
   c. Departure of Paul.   Acts 17: 14.

8. **Paul in Athens.**
   a. Paul's disputation with the philosophers.    Acts 17: 16-21.
   b. The address on Mar's Hill. *Note 6.*    Acts 17: 22-34.
9. **A Year and a Half in Corinth.**
   a. Residence with Aquila and Priscilla.    Acts 18: 1-2.
   b. His trade. *Note 7.*    Acts 18: 3.
   c. Rejoined by Silas and Timothy.    Acts 18: 4-5.
   d. The conversion of Crispus, Gaius. and the Household of Stephanas.    Acts 18: 6-8. I Cor. 1: 14-16. I Cor. 16: 15.
   e. Paul's Vision.    Acts 18: 9-11.
   f. Paul before Gallio.    Acts 18: 12-18.
10. **From Corinth to Ephesus, Cæsarea, Jerusalem and Antioch.**    Acts 18: 18-23.

## NOTES.

1. One reads with regret of the difference that separated two such spirits as Paul and Barnabas. From the meagre account of the difficulty given in the Acts we cannot judge the case. Mark was nephew to Barnabas and the latter was naturally anxious that the consequences of a former separation should not hinder the progress of one whose future must have been promising. Fate decreed that they should meet no more in life, though this was not due to their cherishing any malice toward each other. Paul mentions both Barnabas and Mark with honor and in his last epistle sends for Mark to come to him at Rome, saying he was profitable to him for the ministry, showing that his noble mind no longer cherished a remembrance of the former unpleasantness. The most regrettable result of the incident was that Paul was separated for life from a stalwart friend to whom he owed more than to any other, and Barnabas was deprived of the companionship of one of the noblest of spirits, though in the providence of God this may have been greatly to the benefit of the work.

2. Paul's first purpose in setting forth on this second journey was to visit the brethren in every city where they had preached. The student should here observe the different route followed in this journey. Passing through Syria he visited Tarsus, his home in Cilicia, then passing through the Cilician gates, a narrow defile in the Taurus or Bull mountains, he came to Derbe, the last of the cities visited on his former mission.

3. At first glance there is an apparent inconsistency in the action of Paul in circumcising Timothy after so stoutly contending against the

rite being performed in the case of Titus at the council in Jerusalem; but as stated in the text it was "because of the Jews." Paul was aware that without circumcision the son of a Greek would be powerless to accomplish good among the Jews—in fact without submitting to the rite he would not be permitted to teach in their synagogues—though his mother were a Jewess. In the case of Titus, Paul was contending for a principle, the question of his circumcision having been proposed as a test case.

4. Of all Paul's companions Timothy enjoyed the greatest favor and confidence. From the time of his conversion—probably during Paul's first visit to Lystra—to the end of his career he was intimately associated with the great apostle to the Gentiles, and always retained his warmest friendship. In disposition he was mild and gentle, generous and forgiving, and formed a happy complement to the sturdy character of Paul. We are forced to the conclusion, however, that he was somewhat inclined to indolence, and was not so full of active zeal as Paul would have liked, from the striking admonitions contained in Paul's epistles to him: "Neglect not the gift that is in thee." (1 Timothy, 4: 14); and " Wherefore I put thee in remembrance that thou stir up the gift of God, which is in thee by the putting on of my hands." (2 Timothy, 1: 6.). But this was only one slight fault in a character full of excellent qualities.

5. At this point it will be observed that the narrative changes from the third to the first person plural. From this fact and the additional one that the account from now on is much more minute in detail, we judge that Luke joined the brethren at Troas and described what came under his personal observation.

6. In verse 28 Paul makes reference to the belief in the immortality of the soul, which prevailed among some of the pagans: "As certain also of your own poets have said, For we are also his offspring." Those who through poetic gift or higher powers of thought, were lifted above the common mass of the heathen, had a firm belief in the *natural* immortality of the soul, as the offspring of a God to them unknown. This belief was held and publicly taught by such Greeks as Plato, Aristotle, and especially Socrates and the poet Aratus, whom Paul quotes. Their belief in the immortality of the soul was not dependent upon good works or obedience to any principles. They simply reasoned that, as the offspring of an eternal God, the soul is immortal by its very nature. This is the true view of this matter, as contrasted with the belief held by some, that the immortality of the soul depends upon the righteousness of the individual and his acceptance of the principles of salvation. While the salvation and exaltation of the soul depend upon these, its eternal existence does not.

7. The Jews considered it a religious duty to train their children to some useful occupation. Paul had been taught the art of tent-making as a boy in Tarsus, where the manufacture of tents from the coarse goat hair of the province of Cilicia was a leading occupation. Paul always prided himself on his independence in being able to earn his own bread.

## REVIEW.

1. What led to the difficulty between Paul and Barnabas? 2. Trace on the map Paul's second missionary journey. 3. What were the probable reasons for circumcising Timothy? 4. What was the nature of Paul's vision at Troas? 5. Where is Troas? 6. What reasons are there for thinking that Luke joined the missionaries at Troas? 7. Give a brief account of their labors in Philippi. 8. Where is Thessalonica. 9. By whom was Paul opposed in Thessalonica? 10. Where is Berea? 11. For what was Athens especially noted? 12. What schools of philosophy did Paul encounter there? 13. What was the nature of the philosophy of each?

# LESSON X.

## PAUL'S THIRD MISSIONARY JOURNEY.

| EVENTS. (A. D. 54-58.) | REFERENCES. |
|---|---|
| 1. Paul revisits the churches of Galatia and Phrygia. | Acts 18: 22-23. |
| 2. The work of Apollos in Ephesus. | Acts 18: 24-28. |
| 3. Paul at Ephesus. *Note 1.* | |
|    *a.* Rebaptism of supposed converts. *Note 2.* | Acts 19: 1-7. |
|    *b.* Disputation in the school of Tyrannus. | Acts 19: 8-10. |
|    *c.* Miracles performed. | Acts 19: 11-12. |
|    *d.* Jewish exorcists. *Note 3.* | Acts 19: 13-20. |
|    *e.* Opposition of Demetrius. | Acts 19: 22-41. |
| 4. From Ephesus to Greece. | Acts 20: 1-3. |
| 5. The return Journey. | |
|    *a.* Return through Macedonia to Troas. | Acts 20: 3-12. |
|    *b.* From Troas to Miletus. | Acts 20: 13-16. |
|    *c.* Paul's address at Miletus. | Acts 20: 17-38. |
|    *d.* From Miletus to Tyre. | Acts 21: 1-6. |
|    *e.* To Ptolemais and Cæsarea. The prophecy of Agabus. | Acts 21: 7-15. |
|    *f.* Paul's fifth and last visit to Jerusalem. | Acts 21: 15-16. |

## NOTES.

1. Ephesus was the great commercial metropolis of the Mediterranean on the Asiatic coast. It was not only a commercial, but also a religious center. Here was located the great shrine of the goddess Diana, at which multitudes of devotees came thither to worship. Trades and amusements of all kinds were supported by these great concourses of people, not the least of which was that of the silversmiths, mentioned in the text. They

dealt in miniature models of the goddess, inscribed with symbols and sold to the credulous populace as charms. Paul remained in the city three years, and from the mention of these churches in the Epistles and in Revelation, we judge that the work was quite thoroughly established.

2. This incident furnishes a strong argument for the necessity of baptism before receiving the Holy Ghost, and also for the necessity of the ordinances being performed by one having the proper authority. When Paul found those at Ephesus, who had been baptized, but had not so much as heard of the Holy Ghost, he had good reason to doubt the validity of the baptism they had received and was careful to have them rebaptized before conferring the Holy Ghost. (See Roberts' "The Gospel," page 221).

3. In this incident we have another striking illustration of the necessity of those administering the ordinances of the Gospel, being clothed with proper authority. While the power of Paul became such, that evil spirits were banished by articles of apparel worn by him being brought into their presence, those same spirits would not heed even the name of Jesus when used by those without authority.

"There is a principle of great moment associated with this incident. The question is, if these men, when acting without authority from God, could not drive out an evil spirit, would their administration be of force, or have any virtue in it, had they administered in some other ordinance of the Gospel, say baptism for the remission of sins, or laying on hands for imparting the Holy Ghost? Manifestly it would not. And hence we rightly come to the conclusion, so well expressed in one of our articles of faith, that 'A man must be called of God, by prophecy and by the laying on of hands, by those who are in authority, to preach the gospel and administer in the ordinances thereof.'

"Such a conclusion as this could reasonably be drawn also from the words of Paul, in Hebrews, where he says: 'Every high priest taken from among men is ordained for men in things pertaining to God, that he may offer both gifts and sacrifices for sins. * * * And no man taketh this honor unto himself, but he that is called of God as was Aaron.' (Hebrews 5: 1-5.) The manner in which Aaron was called to the priest's office is recorded in the writings of Moses as follows: 'Take thou unto thee Aaron thy brother, and his sons with him from among the children of Israel, that he may minister unto me in the priest's office, even Aaron, Nadab and Abihu, Eleazar and Ithamar, Aaron's sons.' (Ex. 28: 1.)

"It may be objected that this was the law relating to the calling of high priests alone, but if high priests are to be called in this manner, is it not reasonable to conclude that all who administer in 'things pertaining to God' must be called in the same way—that is, of God? So far as the scriptures are concerned, and on subjects of this character their authority is conclusive, wherever we have an account of men administering in the things pertaining to God, and their administrations are accepted of Him, they have either been called directly by revelation from Him, or through inspiration in those who already had authority from God to act in His name; and to be called by a legitimate, divinely established authority is to be called of God.

"On the other hand, whenever men have taken it upon themselves to act in the name of God, so far as any such instance is recorded, it has been followed by some manifestation of displeasure from Him." (Roberts' "The Gospel," chapter 30.

## REVIEW.

1. Name and locate in their order the places visited by Paul on his third missionary journey. 2. Who was Apollos? 3. For what was Ephesus especially noted? 4. Why did Paul rebaptize those who claimed to have been baptized with John's baptism? 5. How did John's baptism differ from that practiced by Paul? 6. What was the school of Tyrannus? 7. What was the nature of the miracles performed by Paul at Ephesus? 8. What principle of the Gospel is substantiated by the experience of the Jewish exorcists? 9. Who was Demetrius? 10. What length of time did Paul spend in Ephesus? 11. Relate the incidents that happened at Troas during the homeward journey. 12. What warnings did Paul give the elders at Miletus? 13. What was the prophecy of Agabus?

# LESSON XI.

## PAUL'S THIRD MISSIONARY JOURNEY.

| EVENTS. (A. D. 58-60.) | REFERENCES. |
|---|---|

1. **Paul at Ephesus.**
   a. First Epistle to the Corinthians. *Note 1.*  — I Cor. 16: 8.
2. **Journey Through Greece.** — Acts 20: 1-6.
   a. Second Epistle to the Corinthians. *Note 2.*
   b. Epistle to the Romans. *Note 3.*
3. **Paul's Journey Along the Coast of Asia Minor.** *Note 4.*
   a. The miraculous restoration of Eutychus. *Note 5.* — Acts 20: 6-12.
   b. Farewell address to the Saints at Asia. *Note 6.* — Acts 20: 18-36.
   c. Prophecy at Caesarea. *Note 7.* — Acts 21: 8-14.

## NOTES.

1. The first epistle to the Corinthians was written by Paul at Ephesus at the close of his three years' stay in that city, a little before Easter in the year 57 or 58, after he had dispatched Timothy to Corinth and after he had himself resolved to journey through Macedonia and Achaia before going up to Jerusalem. Probably it was the third written of Paul's epistles, being preceded by I. and II. Thessalonians. (See Bagster's Bible Helps.)

2. This epistle was written a short time after the first, but from Macedonia, whither Paul had gone to meet Titus whom he had sent before him to ascertain the condition of affairs in the Corinthian church. It may be well to observe the change of style from reproachful sadness to hopeful gladness and commendation that follows the report of Titus. (2

Cor. 7: 3.) This is valuable in showing how even inspired men put their feelings into writing. Every letter, public speech or book is a reflex of the spiritual condition of the writer.

3. The epistle of the Romans is generally believed to be the sixth of Paul's epistles and was written from Corinth, which was the Roman capital of Greece, to the Christian church at Rome. This church appears to have consisted originally of Jews and Jewish proselytes, who had been early converted to Christianity and had settled at Rome. There were two errors of fundamental importance against which it was necessary he should at once caution the church at Rome, and it was to correct these errors that he wrote his epistle. It had come to his ears that the Jewish Christians, on the one hand, challenged the equal rights of the Gentiles, as such, to the privileges of the Gospel: and the Gentile Christians on the other, regarded the rejection of the Jews as their final exclusion from God's kingdom; and he wrote this epistle partly to show that the one had no more right to the grace of God than the other, and that this grace contemplates the final conversion of the Jew as well as the Gentile.

4. From Corinth. Paul and his friends journeyed overland through Greece and Macedonia, to Philippi (Acts 20: 3-6) a place now visited for the third time. Here Paul was rejoined by Luke the Evangelist, who henceforth shared his dangers to the end of his life. Most of Paul's company sailed from Philippi across the Aegean sea to Troas, in advance of the apostle, but were soon followed by Paul and Luke. (Acts 20: 5-13). At Troas they remained for a week with the church; and here Eutychus was restored to life by the apostle. From Philippi most of the company set sail for Palestine, but Paul went on foot as far as Assos, where he was taken on board (Acts 20: 13-14.) This place was situated 19 miles from Troas and is now marked by extensive ruins.

Mitylene. This was on the island of Lesbos, famed as the home of Sappho, the Greek poetess. Here they anchored for the night, as the channel was not easy to follow among the islands (Acts 20:14.) This and the succeeding stations in the Aegean Sea may be noticed on the map of the islands and coasts of Asia Minor.

Chios. (Acts 20: 15.) This is an island near the mainland, 42 miles southwest of Smyrna; and 27 miles long. It was the birthplace of the philosopher Pythagoras. They barely touched at the island and then sailed across to the shore of Asia Minor.

Trogyllium (Acts 20:15) is a town and cape on the coast of Asia Minor at the foot of Mount Mycale. The place at which they anchored for the night is still called St. Paul's Port. On the next day they sailed past the harbor of Ephesus without stopping, for Paul's stations were controlled by the movements of the ship and its masters.

Miletus. (Acts 20: 16-38). This was at the mouth of the river Maeander, 35 miles south of Ephesus; and at that time on the shore though now ten miles inland by the changes on the coast. Here, while the ship was delayed, Paul sent for the elders of the church at Ephesus, and gave to them a farewell addresss of deep tenderness. This place is now a small village, called Melas.

Rhodes (Acts 21: 1), is an island of note in both ancient and modern history, 13 miles from Asia Minor, 46 miles long, and 18 wide. Upon it had stood the Colossus, a figure over 100 feet high, but overthrown by an earthquake, B. C. 224, and prostrate at the time of Paul's visit.

Patara (Acts 21: 1) was a seaport in the province of Lycia, in Asia Minor, opposite Rhodes. Here the vessel ended its voyage, and the apostolic company found another, which was bound for Phœnicia. The place is now a ruin and is buried in the encroaching sand.

The disciples took another ship at Patara and sailed in a southeasterly direction for Phœnicia, passing by Cyprus without stopping. The vessel paused for a week at Tyre to unlade its burden, and here Paul found a church, perhaps planted by Philip the evangelist. Tyre had once been the great commercial metropolis of the Mediterranean, known as the "strong city" as early as the time of Joshua. It was the capital of Phœnicia, and in Old Testament times held friendly relations with Israel, but was idolatrous and abominably wicked. It was besieged by Nebuchadnezzar for 13 years, was destroyed by Alexander the Great, rebuilt by the Seleucidae, and, in Paul's time, was still a large city. It is now a miserable village, called Sur, and in the fulfillment of prophecy, "a place for the spreading of nets." (Ezek. 26: 14). Taking ship for the last time, they sailed southward along the coast of Palestine to Ptolemais. (Acts 21: 7). This was the Old Testament Accho, in the tribe of Asher, but never possessed. It was 8 miles north of Mount Carmel. In medieval history it sustained a siege by the Crusaders, and was known as St. Jean d'Acre. Here Paul spent a day with the church, and then journeyed with his friends southward over the plain of Esdraelon and Mount Carmel. At Caesarea, the next station, they were entertained by Philip, who, years before had been driven out of Jerusalem by Saul of Tarsus. Caesarea was the Roman capital of Palestine, and was in all respects a heathen city, though containing many Jews. (Hurlbut's Historical Geography of the Bible.)

5. It was the evening which succeeded the Jewish Sabbath. On the Sunday morning the vessel was about to sail. The Christians of Troas were gathered together at this solemn time to celebrate that feast of love which the last commandment of Christ has enjoined on all His followers. The place was an upper room, with a recess or balcony projecting over the street or court. The night was dark: three weeks had not elapsed since the Passover, and the moon only appeared as a faint crescent in the early part of the night. Many lamps were burning in the room where the congregation was assembled. The place was hot and crowded. St. Paul, with the feeling strongly impressed upon his mind that the next day was the day of his departure, and that souls might be lost by delay, was continuing in earnest discourse and prolonging it even to midnight: when an occurrence suddenly took place, which filled the assembly

with alarm, though it was afterwards converted into an occasion of joy and thanksgiving. A young listener, whose name was Eutychus, was overcome by exhaustion, heat, and weariness, and sank into a deep slumber. He was seated or leaning in the balcony; and, falling down in his sleep, was dashed upon the pavement below, and was taken up dead. Confusion and terror followed with loud lamentation. But Paul was able to exercise the power of that Master whose doctrine he was proclaiming. As Jesus had once said of the young maiden, who was taken by death from the society of her friends, "She is not dead but sleepth," so the Apostle of Jesus received power to restore the dead to life. He went down and fell upon the body like Elisha of old, and, embracing Eutychus, said to the bystanders: "do not lament: for his life is in him." (Conybeare and Howson's Life and Epistles of St. Paul, pp 206, 207.)

Apostle Lund in the Era for July, 1898, states in a letter from Palestine, that a window has been cut in the wall from which tradition states that Eutychus fell.

6. On the arrival at Miletus, some 36 miles south of Ephesus, the vessel was delayed, and Paul not knowing when it would leave, and, therefore, feeling it unsafe to journey to Ephesus, sent word of his presence at Miletus and expressed a desire to meet the officers of the Ephesian church. They hastened with joy to meet their old friend and teacher, whom they had so often heard in the school of Tyrannus. At Miletus, perhaps in some retired spot by the seashore, Paul gave his farewell counsel and instructions, with his usual earnestness and sobriety, intensified by the deepest emotions. His prophetic declaration that he should see them no more brought forth expressions of the reverential love his co-laborers had for him.

It will be observed that while Paul was so solicitous for the progress of the church, he could not forbear, while under the spirit of prophecy, referring to the Apostacy which was to take place. (Acts 20: 29, 30.)

7. At Caesarea Paul was entertained by that Philip whom he had previously persecuted. The fact that Philip's four daughters had been blessed with the gift of prophecy is proof that the foretelling of events was had not among men alone but among faithful women during the apostolic period.

It is not improbable that these inspired women gave Paul some intimation of the sorrows which were hanging over him. But soon a more explicit voice declared the very nature of the trial he was to expect. The stay of the Apostle at Caesarea lasted some days. He had arrived in Judea in good time before the festival and haste was now unnecessary. The news reached Jerusalem of his arrival; and a prophet named Agabus—who also predicted the famine (see Acts 11: 28.)—went down to Caesarea and communicated to Paul and the company of Christians by whom he was surrounded, a clear knowledge of the impending danger. His revelation was made in that dramatic form which impresses the mind with a stronger sense of reality than mere words can do, and which was made familiar to the Jews of old by the practice of the Hebrew prophet. As Isaiah (ch. 20.) loosed the sackcloth from his loins, and put off his shoes from his feet, to declare how the Egyptian captives should be led away into Assyria naked and barefoot,—or as the girdle of Jeremiah (ch. 12.) in its strength and its decay, was made a type of the people of Israel in their privileges and their fall,—Agabus in like manner using the imagery of action, took the girdle of St. Paul, and fastened it around his own hands and feet, and said, "Thus saith the Holy Ghost: so shall the Jews at Jerusalem bind the man to whom this girdle belongs, and they shall deliver him into the hands of the Gentiles." (Conybeare and Howson's Life and Epistles of St. Paul p. 233.)

Instead of hesitating and in spite of the entreaties of his friends, whom the prophecy completely unnerved, Paul declared that he was "ready not only to be bound, but to die at Jerusalem for the name of the Lord Jesus." And then they desisted from their entreaties. Their respect for the Apostle made them silent. They recognized the will of God in the steady purpose of his servant: and gave their acquiescence in those words in which Christian resignation is best expressed : "The will of the Lord be done."

Prophecies are made with the view of preparing one to meet trials in the line of duty, and to warn the wrong doer of the result of the course he will persist in. It gives encouragement and comfort; it instructs, and shows that all things are present with God.

## REVIEW.

1. When and where did Paul write the first epistle to the Corinthians? 2. What was the chief object of the first epistle to the Corinthians? 3. How long did Paul remain in Greece? 4. What Jewish plot was frustrated by Paul in choosing to return through Macedonia instead of taking the more direct route to Jerusalem? 5. Give time and place of writing the second epistle to the Corinthians, and the epistle to the Romans. 6. What was the chief object of the epistle to the Romans? 7 What woman carried Paul's epistle to the Romans? 8. Relate the incident of the miraculous healing at Troas. 9. For what is each of the following places historically famed: Mitylene, Chios, Lamos and Rhodes? 10. Why did not Paul visit Ephesus on his return voyage? 11. For whom did Paul send word to meet him at Miletus? 12. What prediction of Paul filled the saints with grief at Miletus? 13. Give a brief statement of Tyre. (a) what it was, (b) what it is. 14. Give proof from this lesson that women are entitled to the gift of prophecy. 15. Why did Paul's friends at Caesarea entreat him not to go to Jerusalem? 16. What was Paul's reply to the entreaties of his friends at Caesarea? 17. What are the purposes of prophecy?

## LESSON XII.

## PAUL'S LAST VISIT TO JERUSALEM.

EVENTS.  (A. D. 60.)  REFERENCES.

1 Paul's Reception by the Brethren.
   Note 1.
   a. He reports his mission at Jerusalem. — Acts 21:17-19.
   b. Testifies concerning work among the Gentiles. — Acts 21: 19. Rom. 15: 18.
   c. Questioned by his brethren. Note 2. — Acts 21: 20-22. Gal. 5: 3.
   d. In obedience to counsel, he aids in the completion of the ritual of purification. Note 3. — Acts 21: 23-26. Acts 18: 18.

2 Mobbed by Jews and Arrested by Romans.
   a. His presence in the temple arouses Jewish jealousy. — Acts 21: 27.
   b. Charged with heresy and polluting the Temple. Note 4. — Acts 21: 28-29.
   c. In the hands of the mob. — Acts 21: 30-32.
   d. Rescued by the Romans. — Acts 21: 33.
   e. Taken to the castle in custody. — Acts 21: 34.

3 Paul's Defense on the Stairway.
   Note 5.
   a. Declares himself an orthodox Jew. — Acts 22: 3.
   b. Acknowledges his zeal in persecuting the followers of Christ. — Acts 22: 3-5.
   c. Bears testimony to his miraculous conversion. — Acts 22: 6-16.
   d. Declares he was divinely called to preach the Gospel to the Gentiles. — Acts 22: 17-21.

4. **Paul's first Night in the Castle.**
   *Note 6.*
   a. Bound with thongs.     Acts 22: 25-28.
   b. Rescued from scourging.     Acts 22: 29.
5. **Paul before the Jewish Council.**     Acts 22: 30—23: 9.
   a. Ananias prophetically denounced.
   *Note 7.*     Acts 23: 2-3.
   b. Paul's submission to authority.
   *Note 8.*     Acts 23: 4-5.
   c. His accusers divided. *Note 9.*     Acts 23: 6-9.
6. **Paul Rescued by the Roman Guard.**     Acts 23: 10-30.
   a. Protected in the castle. *Note 10.*     Acts 23: 10-11.
   b. Escapes the Jewish plot. *Note 11.*     Acts 23: 12-35.
   d. The Roman captain's official letter.     Acts 23: 26-30.

## NOTES.

1. Evidently Paul had a double object in view in making his journey to Jerusalem; (1.) to report his three years' mission among the Gentiles. (2.) to be present at the Pentecostal feast, which took place fifty days after the Passover and had begun to supplant that feast in the eyes of the Christians. Paul's report was doubtless presented at a council of the priesthood.

2. The opinion prevailed among the converted Jews that Paul had exceeded his authority; had made admission to the church too easy to the Gentiles, and had ignored and spoken against the Mosaic rituals.

3. The Jewish rite of purification consisted entirely of outward observances, the last of which was the shaving of the head to show the expiration of the vow. While as an advocate of inner purification rather than outward ordinances, Paul recognized no necessity for this ordinance, yet he assisted in it as an expediency in obedience to counsel so far as to associate with the four Nazarites and pay the expenses of the ritual.

4. Because Paul had been seen associating with a Greek on the streets the Jews jumped at the conclusion that he had taken the Greek into the temple and so reported it. On the walls of the temple notices were placed warning strangers not to enter the sacred precincts under penalty of death. The Jews, therefore, were not only enraged at Paul, but felt perfectly justified in proceeding to kill him. It was a political necessity for a Roman garrison in the city to suppress riots and other disturbances. It will be remembered that the chief accusers were Jews from Asia with whom Paul had been in controversy on these same questions.

5. The fearlessness of Paul is well depicted here, as well as his confidence in argument and testimony. Especially is manifested the hand of the Lord in thus placing Paul in a position where the greatest enemies of Christianity would be compelled, by force of circumstances, to listen to his testimony. The Jews listened attentively until Paul declared himself a messenger of salvation to the Gentiles. This was more than Jewish intolerance could stand and they sought to wreak immediate vengeance upon him as a heretic and polluter of the temple.

6. Paul was born in Tarsus, where his father had acquired Roman citizenship, which was allowed only to the most worthy of alien subjects. Hence Paul's claim to the privileges of a Roman citizen; but his father in accordance with the custom of wealthy and honorable Jews, gave his son an orthodox education in the theological schools at Jerusalem over which Gamaliel presided. In Tarsus Greek was the accepted language. It was also the language of commerce. Probably Paul acquired the Hebrew vernacular in the domestic circle, while in social life he used the Greek.

7. This hypocritical president of the Sanhedrim, Ananias, was killed during the Jewish war with the Romans.

8. Paul exhibited proper respect for constituted authority, notwithstanding the fact that the man who claimed to hold it was a despot. Evidently Paul could entertain no other feeling than that of contempt for he person who would sit as a judge under the law, yet issue an order contrary to the law, but he bowed in submission to the divine principle of proper respect for constituted authority. The Lord Jesus also gave an example of this in providing tribute money for the entrance into Capernaum. See Matt. 17: 24-27. The conduct of David in refusing to harm his persecutor, King Saul, when the latter sought his life, affords another instance. See I Sam. 24-26.

9. The Pharisees, to which sect Paul had belonged, represented the cultured and progressive class of Jews and believed in redemption, resurrection, and final judgment, while the Sadducees were the agnostics of that age.

10. The Lord not only commands to visit those who are in prison, but He sets the example himself. At the very time when He was assuring Paul of his safety, forty emissaries of the evil one pitted their puny human will against the divine will and bound themselves by oath to assassinate God's chosen messenger. The result was as it always will be—defeat for the devil, victory for Christ. When one contemplates the folly of these men, he is led to see plainly that wickedness and wisdom are never companions. See President Cannon's Life of Joseph Smith, chap. 28.

## REVIEW.

1. What were the two main objects of Paul's coming to Jerusalem?
2. Why were the church officials at Jerusalem so desirous of having Paul speak to the converted Jews at an early date? 3. What was the object of having Paul aid in the Mosaic ritual of purification before he presented

himself to the public? 4. On what grounds was Paul accused as a defiler of the temple? 5. How can you account for his accusers being Jews from Asia? 6. What evidence have we that the Roman rule at Jerusalem was a necessity at this time? 7. Why did Paul address the mob in the Hebrew language and the Roman officer in the Greek? 8. How came Paul to be a Roman citizen? 9. Show the distinction between submitting to men and submitting to constituted authority. 10. What object had Paul in declaring himself a Pharisee when on trial before the Jewish council. 11. In what respect are all true Christians Pharisees? 12. What evidence have we that this trial was in a public or open court? 13. What appears to have been the chief object of the angel's visit to Paul in the castle? 14. How came the Roman officer to be so deeply concerned in Paul's welfare? 15. Show from this lesson the futility of putting human will against divine will.

## LESSON XIII.

## PAUL AT CAESAREA.

| EVENTS. (A. D. 60-62.) | REFERENCES. |
|---|---|
| 1. **Examination before Felix.** | |
|    *a.* The accusation by the Jews. *Note 1.* | Acts 24: 1-9. |
|    *b.* Paul's answer to the charges. *Note 2.* | Acts 24: 10-21. |
|    *c.* Indefinite postponement of trial. *Note 3.* | Acts 24: 22. |
| 2. **Two years in custody.** | Acts 24: 23-27. |
|    *a.* Paul's conversation with Felix and Drusilla. *Note 4.* | Acts 24: 22-27. |
| 3. **Paul accused before Festus.** | |
|    *a.* The petition of the Jews for Paul to be tried at Jerusalem. | Acts 25: 1-6. |
|    *b.* His appeal to Cæsar. | Acts 25: 11. |
|    *c.* His examination before Festus. *Note 5.* | Acts 25: 7-12. |
| 4. **Paul's hearing before King Agrippa.** | |
|    *a.* The political visit of Agrippa and Bernice to Festus. *Note 6.* | Acts 25: 13-27. |
|    *b.* Festus' ceremonious address. | Acts 25: 24-27. |
|    *c.* Paul's defence. *Note 7.* | Acts 26: 1-29. |
|    *d.* The judges convinced of truth. *Note 8.* | Acts 26: 30-32. |
|    *e.* Paul ordered to be sent to Rome. *Note 9.* | |

### NOTES.

1. The law required that cases should be heard speedily; and the apostle's enemies in Jerusalem were not wanting in zeal. Thus, "after five days," the high priest Ananias and certain members of the Sanhedrim, appeared with one of those advocates who practised in the law courts of the provinces, where the forms of Roman law were imperfectly known, and the Latin language imperfectly understood. The man whose

professional services were engaged on this occasion was called Tertullus. The name is Roman and there is little doubt that he was an Italian, and spoke on this occasion in Latin. The incriminating information was formally laid before the governor. The prisoner was summoned and Tertullus brought forward the charges against him in a set speech, which we need not quote at length. He began by loading Felix with unmerited praises, and then proceeded to allege three distinct heads of accusation against Paul; charging him first with causing factious disturbances among all the Jews throughout the empire (which was an offence against the Roman government, and amounted to *Majestas* or treason against the emperor), secondly, with being a ring leader of "the sect of the Nazarenes," (which involved heresy against the law of Moses), and thirdly, with an attempt to profane the temple at Jerusalem, (an offence not only against the Jewish, but also against the Roman law, which protected the Jews in the exercise of their worship). He concluded by asserting (with serious deviations from the truth) that Lysias, the commandant of the garrison, had forcibly taken the prisoner away, when the Jews were about to judge him by their own ecclesiastical law, and had thus improperly brought the matter before Felix. The drift of this representation was evidently to pursuade Felix to give up Paul to the Jewish courts, in which case his assassination would have easily been accomplished. And the Jews who were present gave a vehement assent to the statements of Tertullus, making no secret of their animosity against Paul, and asserting that these things were indeed so. *Conybeare & Howson's Life and Epistles of St. Paul, page 282.* This incident illustrates the fact that envy and hatred are emotions which impel men to the accomplishment of evil, nearly, if not quite as strongly, as love impels them to good.

2. And the Apostle after briefly expressing his satisfaction that he had to plead his cause before one so well acquainted with Jewish customs, refuted Tertullus step by step. He said that on his recent visit to Jerusalem at the festival (and he added that it was only "twelve days" since he had left Caesarea for that purpose), he had caused no disturbance in any part of Jerusalem; that, as to heresy, he had never swerved from his belief in the law and the prophets, and that in conformity with that belief, he held the doctrine of a resurrection, and sought to live conscientiously before the God of his fathers; and as to the temple, so far from profaning it he had been found in it deliberately observing the very strictest ceremonies. The Asiatic Jews, he added, who had been his first accusers, ought to have been present as witnesses now. Those who were present knew full well that no other charge was brought home to him before the Sanhedrim, except what related to the belief that he held in common with the Pharisees. *Conybeare & Howson's Life and Epistles of St. Paul, page 283.*

3. Paul's words harmonized entirely with the statement contained in the dispatch of Claudius Lysias. Moreover, Felix had resided so long in Caesarea, where the Christian religion had been known for many years,

and had penetrated even among the troops, "that he had a more accurate knowledge of their religion" (v. 22) than to be easily deceived by the misrepresentations of the Jews. Thus a strong impression was made on the mind of this wicked man. But his was one of those characters, which are easily affected by feelings, but always drawn away from right action by the overpowering motive of self-interest. He could not make up hi mind to acquit Paul. He deferred all inquiry into the case for the present "When Lysias comes down." he said, "I will decide finally between you." Meanwhile he placed him under the charge of the centurion who had brought him to Cæsarea, with directions that he should be treated with kindness and consideration. Close confinement was indeed necessary, both to keep him in safety from the Jews, and because he was not yet acquitted, but orders were given that he should have every relaxation which could be allowed in such a case, and that any of his friends should be allowed to visit him, and to minister to his comfort. *Conybeare & Howson's Life and Epistles of St. Paul, page 285.*

4. We are explicitly informed why the governor shut his ears to conviction, and even neglected his official duty, and kept his prisoner in cruel suspense. "He hoped that he might receive from Paul a bribe for his liberation." He was not the only governor of Judea, against whom a similar accusation is brought; and Felix, well knowing how Christians aided one another in distress, and possibly having some information of the funds with which Paul had been recently entrusted, and ignorant of those principles which make it impossible for a true Christian to tamper by bribes with the course of the law, might naturally suppose that he had here a good prospect of enriching himself. "Hence, he frequently sent for Paul and had many conversations with him." But his hopes were unfulfilled: Paul, who was ever ready to claim the protection of the law, would not seek to evade it by dishonorable means: and the Christians who knew how to pray for an apostle in bonds (Acts 12), would not forget the duty of "rendering unto Cæsar the things that are Cæsar's." Thus Paul remained in the Prætorium: and the suspense continued "two years." *Conybeare & Howson's Life and Epistles of St. Paul, page 287.* Felix was a Roman freedman, brother of Pallas, the emperor's favorite. He obtained his high position by means of his successful expeditions against the robbers of the desert, and married Drusilla, the daughter of the tyrant Herod Agrippa I, and sister of Agrippa II and Bernice. He was a man of voluptuous and brutal character, exercising, as Tacitus tells us, the power of a king with the temper of a slave. The effect of Paul's fearless testimony to the truth before Felix, affords a fine illustration of how vice quails before virtue, though the former be shielded by official dignity and the latter stands in the attitude of a chained prisoner.

During the two years in which Paul lay in prison, Jewish dissatisfaction ripened into an outbreak in which thousands of Jews were slain. As a result Felix was summoned to Rome to answer for maladministration and Festus was appointed in his place.

5. Festus was met by a request that Paul be brought to Jerusalem for a trial before the Sanhedrim. But the real purpose was to assassinate him. The answer of Festus was dignified and just and worthy of his office. He said that Paul was in custody at Cæsarea, and that he himself was shortly to return thither, adding that it was not the custom of the Romans to give up an uncondemned prisoner as a mere favor. The accused must have the accuser face to face, and full opportunity must be given for a defence. Those, therefore, who were competent to undertake the task of accusers should come down with him to Cæsarea and there prefer the accusation. Festus remained "eight or ten days" in Jerusalem and then returned to Cæsarea, and the accusers went down the same day. No time was lost after their arrival. The very next day Festus took his seat on the judicial tribunal with his assessors near him and ordered Paul to be brought before him. "The Jews who had come down from Jerusalem" stood round, bringing various heavy accusations against him (which, however, they could not establish), and clamorously asserted that he was worthy of death. We must not suppose that the charges now brought were different in substance from those urged by Tertullus. The prosecutors, in fact, were the same now as then, namely, delegates from the Sanhedrim; and the prisoner was still lying under the former accusation, which had never been withdrawn. We see from what is said of Paul's defence that the charges were still classed under the same heads as before, viz: Heresy, sacrilege, and treason. But Festus saw very plainly that Paul's offence was really connected with the religious opinion of the Jews, instead of relating, as he at first suspected, to some political movement; and he was soon convinced that he had done nothing worthy of death. Being, therefore, in perplexity and at the same time desirous of ingratiating himself with the provincials, he proposed to Paul that he should go up to Jerusalem and be tried there in his presence, or at least under his protection. But the apostle knew full well the danger that lurked in his proposal, and conscious of the rights which he possessed as a Roman citizen, he refused to accede to it, and hence his memorable appeal to Cæsar. *Conybeare & Howson's Life and Epistles of St. Paul, page 290.*

6. It happened that about this time Herod Agrippa II, King of Chalcis, with his sister Bernice, came on a complimentary visit to the new governor and "stayed some days" at Cæsarea. This prince had been familiarly acquainted from his youth with all that related to the Jewish law, and moreover was at this time (as we have seen) superintendent of the Temple with the power of appointing the high priest. Festus took advantage of this opportunity of consulting one better informed than himself on the points in question. He recounted to Agrippa what has summarily been related above, confessing his ignorance of Jewish theology, and alluding especially to Paul's reiterated assertion concerning "one Jesus who had died and was alive again." This cannot have been the first time that Agrippa had heard of the resurrection of Jesus or of the Apostle Paul. His curiosity was aroused and he expressed a wish to see the

prisoner. Festus readily acceded to the request and fixed the next day for the interview. At the time appointed Agrippa and Bernice came with great pomp and display and entered into the audience-chamber with a suite of military officers and the chief men of Caesarea; and at the command of Festus Paul was brought before him. The proceedings were opened by a ceremonious speech from Festus himself, describing the circumstances under which the prisoner had been brought under his notice, and ending with a statement of his perplexity as to what he should write to "his Lord" the Emperor. This being concluded, Agrippa said condescendingly to Paul that he was now permitted to speak for himself. *Conybeare & Howson's Life and Epistles of St. Paul, page 294.*

7. Paul's defence is a model of oratory, moving as it did those who were opposed to Christianity and to Paul himself. The introduction, calculated to remove prejudice, is filled with respectful consideration. Paul recognized in Agrppia a man skilled in Jewish law and tradition and not a stranger to Christianity. Then followed the straightforward, fearless testimony of his conversion which had effected more conversions than had many learned arguments. It appears an illustration of the fact that testimony of the truth is something that a man both knows and feels and in the case of bearing testimony, these two channels of mental and spiritual power sweep before them objections that could not be removed by appealing to the intellect alone. Through the power of testimony men are made to feel the truth, and Agrippa evidently felt the truth of Christianity when, forgetful of his dignity and the differences between Jewish and Christian orthodoxy, he exclaimed: "Almost thou persuadest me to be a Christian."

8. Conviction of the truth often comes to those who are too cowardly or too wrapped up in this world to take a bold stand for what they know to be right.

9. In this case Festus and Agrippa were spared the necessity of action. The appeal to Caesar had been made. There was no retreat for either Festus or Paul. On the new governor's part there was no wish to continue the procrastination of Felix; and nothing now remained but to wait for a convenient opportunity of sending his prisoner to Rome.

## REVIEW.

1. Who was Felix? 2. On what grounds was the accusation of Tertullus based? 3. Why did Paul in his defence lay such stress upon the subject of the resurrection? 4. Upon what grounds did Felix indefinitely postpone the trial? 5. In what manner did Paul pass his two years' captivity in Caesarea? 6. Why was Felix removed from his official position? 7. Why did the Jews wish Paul sent to Jerusalem for trial? 8. Why did Paul appeal to Caesar? 9. Who were Agrippa and Bernice? 10. Why did Festus refer the hearing to King Agrippa? 11. Of what does testimony consist? 12. Show the value of personal testimony in con-

version. 13. What was the effect of Paul's defence upon his auditors? 14. Upon what grounds did Paul appeal to Caesar? 15. What was the effect of an appeal to Caesar? 16. What was the testimony of Festus and Agrippa as to Paul's guilt or innocence of the charge preferred against him?

# LESSON XIV.

## PAUL'S VOYAGE TO ROME.

| EVENTS. (A. D. 62.) | REFERENCES. |
|---|---|
| 1. From the Embarkation to the Shipwreck. | |
|    *a.* The evening of freedom at Sidon. *Note 1.* | Acts 27: 3. |
|    *b.* Change of vessels at Myra. *Note 2.* | Acts 27: 5-6. |
|    *c.* Paul's warning at the Fair Havens. *Note 3.* | Acts 27: 8-10. |
|    *d.* Promise of safety in the midst of peril. *Note 4.* | Acts 27: 11-26. |
| 2. The Shipwreck | |
|    *a.* The attempted desertion. *Note 5.* | Acts 27: 27-32. |
|    *b.* Breaking of the fast. *Note 6.* | Acts 27: 33-37. |
|    *c.* Casting out the cargo and running ship aground. | Acts 27: 38-41. |
|    *d.* Prisoners saved from execution. *Note 7.* | Acts 27: 43. |
|    *e.* Paul's prediction fulfilled. | Acts 27: 44. |
| 3. At Melita. *Note 8.* | |
|    *a.* The hospitable inhabitants. | Acts 28: 1-2. |
|    *b.* The miracle at the camp fire. *Note 9.* | Acts 28: 3-6. |
|    *c.* Entertained by Publius. *Note 10.* | Acts 28: 7-10. |
| 4. Completion of the Journey. | |
|    *a.* The voyage resumed. *Note 11.* | Acts 28: 11-14. |
|    *b.* Welcomed at Appii Forum. *Note 12.* | Acts 28: 15. |
|    *c.* Arrival at Rome. *Note 13.* | Acts 28: 16. |

## NOTES.

1. Julius the centurion, in whose custody Paul was placed with other prisoners, seems to have been somewhat acquainted with the true character of the Apostle so far at least as to feel safe in trusting to his honor; so he gave him perfect liberty to visit his friends unguarded.

2. Sidon was the capital of Phœnicia and after the destruction of Tyre by Alexander the Great became the most important seaport of the Syrian coast. Many ships from different ports had taken refuge at Myra and among the number Julius found one which had come from Alexandria with a cargo of wheat, and was soon to sail for Italy. He immediately had his prisoners transferred to it and they, with the persons previously on board, made a company of 276. We are apt to imagine the vessels of that time as small, and so doubtless many of them were, but this one to have accommodated so many must have been comparatively large, and it is supposed from many known facts that the burden of some ancient merchantmen may have been from 500 to 1000 tons. *Child's History of Paul.*

3. Here we have an example of the so-called scientific knowledge or wisdom coming in conflict with revelation. It was quite natural or rather human for the centurion to have more confidence in the opinion of the navigators than in the declaration of the tent-maker and preacher. The Roman could not understand God's method of imparting knowedge.

4. Authority on the vessel is about to change hands. Note the wonderful declaration of the angel, saying: "Lo, God hath given thee all that sail with thee!" Can it be doubted that Paul had been pleading before the Father in the name of Jesus for both crew and passengers?

5. Man is prone when his wisdom has failed, to take the shortest cut out of the difficulty into which his folly has led him; but those who know that God's wisdom can not fail are able to "stand still and see the salvation of the Lord,"—it generally takes more will power to wait than it does to work. Here the civil authority on the ship had weakened. The military was at a loss what to do. The ecclesiastical furnished the source of safety, as it did in the days when statesmen and warriors *counseled* with men of divine inspiration.

6. In this hour of anxiety the Apostle stands forward to give them courage. He reminds them that they had eaten nothing for 14 days and exhorts them now to partake of a hearty meal, pointing out to them that this was indeed essential to their safety, and encouraging them by the assurance that "not a hair of their heads should perish." So speaking he set the example of the cheerful use of God's gifts and grateful acknowledgements of the giver by taking bread, giving thanks to God before all and beginning to eat. The fast occurred in the month Tisri, early in October, and was the period in which the most violent storms swept the Mediterranean.

7. The soldiers who were answerable with their lives for the detention of their prisoners were afraid lest some of them should swim out and

escape, and, therefore, in the spirit of Roman cruelty, they proposed to kill them at once.

8. Melita corresponds to the modern Malta. It was then inhabited sparsely by semi-civilized descendants of Phœnician colonists. The people were noted for their hospitality.

9. Evidently the same promises and blessings were given to the former day ministers of the Gospel, as to the authorized ones of modern times. See Doc. & Cov. Sec. 84: 62-75. This was the second opportunity that Paul had of receiving the homage due to Divinity alone, but he honestly and wisely gave the superstitious people to understand that the power was not in him and that he was their fellow-man. Paul's conduct in this regard is in marked contrast with that of Herod the Great, who accepted honors not due him, and was smitten to death by the power whose authority he had tacitly usurped.

10. The healing power of the holy priesthood was effectually exercised among the simple, superstitious people. The circumstances point to the comprehensiveness of the promise "the prayer of faith shall heal the sick." It is not limited or circumscribed by social standing or creed fellowship. This should settle the question as to whether non-members of the church can be administered to if they manifest belief in the ordinance.

11. Castor and Pollux were the heathen divinities who were supposed to preside over the fortunes of sailors, hence the name of the ship.

12. Julius, who had become deeply interested in Paul, wished to make him as comfortable as possible, and when his friends desired him to remain with them seven days, the officers readily consented.

13. Paul's approach had been heralded at Rome, and when he arrived at Appii Forum, a town about 40 miles from the great metropolis, several of the brethren met and welcomed him. At the three taverns a second delegation was met, who had also come out to welcome this ambassador in bonds. It was along this Appii Forum road by which Paul entered Rome that he was led forth some years later to his execution.

14. We may well conclude that Julius would speak well of Paul as he delivered him up to the prefect of the pretorian guards. Festus, before whom he had been lately tried at Caesarea, was also in Rome and may have spoken in his favor and thus Providence brought it about that Paul was not cast into the common prison, but was permitted to live in his own hired house, guarded only by a Roman soldier.

## REVIEW.

1. What was a centurion? 2. What two disciples were Paul's companions on this voyage? 3. How can you account for Paul's courteous treatment by Julius? 4. Where is Sidon and for what is it historically noted? 5. Why did they change ships at Myra? 6. Speak of the cargo and the capacity of the vessel in which Paul embarked at Myra. 7. Show

from this lesson that human wisdom cannot compete with divine wisdom. 8. Prove by scriptural quotation that Paul obtained a promise through fasting and prayer. 9. Contrast the conduct of the ship's crew with modern seamen. 10. Why were the Romans anxious to slay their prisoners? 11. Locate Melita and give its modern name. 12. What is said in the Doctrine and Covenants about boasting of spiritual power and protection? 13. Through what documents must the Christians at Rome have become acquainted with Paul? 14. Tell of the meeting at Appii Forum. 15. Why was Paul not sent to the common prison?

# LESSON XV.

## EPISTLES WRITTEN FROM ROME.

| NAMES OF EPISTLES. (A. D. 63-64.) *Note 1.* | REFERENCES. |
|---|---|
| 1. **Ephesians.** | Acts 18: 19. |
|    *a.* Who the Ephesians were. *Note 2.* | Acts 19. |
| | Acts 20: 16-38. |
|    *b.* Purpose of the Epistle. *Note 3.* | 1 Cor. 15: 32. |
| | 1 Tim. 1: 3. |
|    *c.* Its principal contents. *Note 4.* | Ephesians. |
| 2. **Colossians.** | Colossians. |
|    *a.* The church at Colossæ. *Note 5.* | |
|    *b.* Object in writing the Epistle. *Note 6.* | |
|    *c.* Subjects treated. *Note 7.* | Acts 16: 12-40. |
| 3. **Philippians.** | Philippians. |
|    *a.* History of the church at Philippi. *Note 8.* | |
|    *b.* Object of the Epistle. *Note 9.* | |
|    *c.* Contents. *Note 10.* | |
| 4. **Philemon.** | Philemon. |
|    *a.* Who Philemon was. *Note 11.* | |
|    *b.* Purpose and nature of the Epistle. *Note 12.* | |

## NOTES.

1. The dates given are merely approximate, as it is not definitely known in what year Paul reached Rome, or in what portion of his stay there the epistles were written.

2. It is the intention that under this branch of each topic, a brief history of the church or person addressed in the epistle shall be given, by way of gaining a better understanding of the reasons for Paul's writing the epistles, its contents, etc. This information may be obtained in part from the references given above, as also from Oxford or Bagster's Bible helps, Smith's Bible Dictionary or Kitto's Cyclopedia of Biblical Literature. There is supposed to be no definite reason for the claim made by some commentators, that this was a circular letter, addressed to all the churches through-

out Asia Minor. The church at Ephesus was established mainly through the efforts of Paul during his second and third missionary journeys. It was especially during his second visit to the city that many converts were made, the craft of the silversmiths being endangered to such an extent that they raised a tumult, which was quelled by the wisdom and presence of mind of the town clerk (Acts 19). In Paul's return from his third missionary journey he did not visit Ephesus. but sent for the elders of the church there to meet him at Miletus (Acts 20: 17-38). He left Timothy in charge of the church there (1 Tim. 1: 3), and there is a tradition that the Apostle John spent the later years of the century at Ephesus.

3. The object of this epistle seems to have been to show the equal right of the Gentiles with the Jews, to the benefits of Christianity, and to explain the perfect unity of the church.

4. In the first three chapters are words of encouragement and exhortation to the Gentiles. In the fourth, the unity of the church is likened to that of the body, and the officers of the church are particularized. The remainder of the epistle deals with exhortation to duties of obedience and purity. (Read especially 4: 3-16).

5. It seems that Paul had never visited Colossae, the church there having been established by some one else, probably Epaphras (Col. 1: 7; 4: 12). It consisted of Jews and Gentiles; its subsequent history is dim and uncertain. No great doubt as to the genuineness of this epistle as a production of Paul has been raised by the critics.

(This epistle and the others should be carefully read and the review questions thoroughly answered.)

6. This epistle was written on account of the danger of apostasy by the Colossians, and to correct certain errors, leading to the neglect and mortification of the body.

7. The atonement of Christ is magnified in the first chapter: in the second and third the people are exhorted to put away certain sins and perform faithfully the various duties of life.

8. The Church at Philippi was founded by Paul, with Silas, Luke, and Timothy, during his second missionary journey (Acts 16.). The first European conversions to Christianity were made here, three notable converts being Lydia, a dealer in the purple: a Greek divining girl; and the Roman jailor, with his family. The church at Philippi seems to have remained faithful for a longer time than any of the others, and to have entertained a lasting respect for Paul and his apostolic authority. The genuineness of this epistle has never been called into serious question.

9. The Epistle to the Philippians was occasioned by his gratitude for certain gifts sent him by the Philippians.

10. No particular doctrine is advanced, but the Philippians are exhorted to faith and unity in Christ.

11. Philemon was a convert of Paul, living at Colossae and keeping "open house" for the missionaries who visited that city.

12. A slave of Philemon, Onesimus by name, had run away with some of his master's property, and gone to Rome. Here Paul met him, converted him to Christianity and sent him back to Philemon as a "brother beloved," commending him to the Christian care and solicitude of his master. The epistle is, therefore, purely a personal one. This epistle has been universally admired as a model of graceful, delicate, manly writing. "It is a voucher," says Eichhorn, "for the Apostle's urbanity, politeness and knowledge of the world. His advocacy of Onesimus is of the most insinuating and persuasive character, and yet without the slightest perversion or concealment of any fact. The errors of Onesimus are admitted, as was necessary, lest the just indignation of his master against him should be roused anew; but they are alluded to in the most admirable manner; the good side of Onesimus is brought to view, but in such a way as to facilitate the friendly reception of him by his master, as a consequence of Christianity, to which he had, during his absence, been converted; and his future fidelity is vouched for by the noble principles of Christianity."—*Kitto.*

## REVIEW.

1. What was the length of Paul's stay in Rome? 2. Give the date, as nearly as it is known. 3. Name the epistles he wrote during this period. (See next lesson). 4. Who where the Ephesians? 5. Where was their city? 6. Who founded the church there? 7. At what time was this done? 8. Name one incident which occurred in Ephesus during Paul's second visit. 9. Where did the Ephesian elders meet Paul on his return from his third missionary journey? 10. Who was left in charge of the church at Ephesus? 11. What can you say of John's connection with that city? 12. What was Paul's object in writing the epistle to the Ephesians? 13. Explain chapter 1, verse 10. 14. Chapter 2, verses 20-22. 15. What apt comparison is used in the fourth chapter? 16. What officers are named in this chapter? 17. What was the object of their appointment? 18. What exhortations are given in the fifth chapter? 19. What weapons and armor of righteousness are named in the sixth chapter? 20. Where was Colossae? 21. Through whom was the church established there? 22. Why did Paul write to the Colossians? 23. What testimony of Christ is given in the first chapter? 24. What is said regarding the Atonement? 25. What warning is given in the second chapter? 26. What beautiful figure regarding baptism? 27. Repeat the chief exhortations of the third chapter. 28. Where was Philippi? 29. For what is it noted in Christian history? 30. Name some notable conversions which occurred there. 31. By whom were these persons converted? 32. Why did Paul write to the Philippians? 33. What are the main contents of the epistle? 34. Who was Philemon? 35. Who was Onesimus? 36. Why did Paul write to Philemon? 37. Why is this called a personal epistle? 38. What are its main contents? 39. What do the critics say of it? 40. What phase of Paul's character does it illustrate?

## LESSON XVI.

## EPISTLES WRITTEN FROM ROME.—(Concluded.)

| NAMES OF EPISTLES. | (A. D. 63-64). | REFERENCES. |
|---|---|---|
| 1. I and II Timothy. | | Acts 16: 1-3.<br>Acts 17: 14-16.<br>Romans 16: 21.<br>1 Cor. 16: 10.<br>2 Cor. 1: 1-19.<br>Phil. 2: 19.<br>I Thess. 3: 2.<br>Hebrews 13: 23.<br>1 and 2 Timothy. |

    *a.* Account of Timothy. *Note 1.*
    *b.* Why Epistles were written to him. *Note 2.*
    *c.* Contents of the Epistles. *Note 3.*

| | | |
|---|---|---|
| 2. Titus. | | 2 Cor. 2: 13.<br>2 Cor. 7: 6-13-15.<br>2 Cor. 8: 16-18-23.<br>2 Cor. 12: 18.<br>Gal. 2: 3.<br>2 Timothy 4: 10.<br>Titus. |

    *a.* Account of Titus. *Note 4.*
    *b.* Object of the Epistle.
    *c.* Its contents. *Note 5.*

3. Hebrews.                            Hebrews.

    *a.* To whom addressed. *Note 6.*
    *b.* General analysis. *Note 7.*

## NOTES.

1. Timothy was the son of a Jewess by a Greek father. Paul conceived an early liking for him, which lasted until the apostle's death. He accompanied Paul on one of his missionary tours, and, it is supposed, was with him during a portion of his imprisonment at Rome. Timothy is supposed to have become, subsequently, Bishop of Ephesus, and to have met a martyr's death in that city.

2. The Epistles were written to Timothy on account of his having been left in charge of the church at Ephesus, and his need of instructions

regarding his duties. The second may have been written by Paul shortly before his death, as a sort of farewell exhortation. These two Epistles and the one to Titus are called pastoral, for the reason that the ones addressed were in charge of branches of the church, or, figuratively, were "pastors of the flock of Christ," and the Epistles were intended to instruct them in their duties.

3. In the First Epistle Paul speaks of the universality of the Gospel, the duties of men in public prayer, and the proper place and order of women. He then particularizes the duties of men in authority, especially with reference to false teachers, whose rise is predicted. (Thess. 4: 1-11.) This is a striking and remarkable prediction of the apostasy of the primitive church. Not only is the rise of false teachers predicted, but even the doctrines they were to advance. The most serious feature of the prophecy is the statement that these deceivers were to be professed believers in Christ, their light being changed to darkness. The consequences of their false teaching would be much more disastrous to the church than if they had never been members. If Paul had read the history of the ten centuries subsequent to his time, he could scarcely have portrayed this feature of the apostasy more clearly and concisely. The remainder of the Epistle is taken up with general instructions and exhortations. In the second, the steadfastness and faithfulness of Timothy are mentioned and commended, and his course is contrasted with that of the false teachers and ungodly men who had already risen. Referring to his own approaching departure Paul exhorts Timothy to increased faithfulness and diligence.

4. Titus was converted by Paul probably in his first missionary journey and was his companion in many of his labors and dangers, including his final visit to the churches and his stay at Rome. Titus is said to have returned thence to Crete, where he acted as bishop until his death.

5. This Epistle, written to instruct Titus in the duties of his bishopric, contains directions regarding the necessary qualifications of those whom he should call to the ministry, and the proper performance of his own duties. In the first chapter a hint of the progress of the apostasy is given, in Paul's statement of the evil teachings and deeds of professed Christians. In the second, the duties of the saints of all ages and conditions are given, and Titus is instructed to exhort his people to a proper performance of these duties. The last chapter is occupied with warnings and admonitions against sin.

6. There has been a great deal of discussion as to who are addressed in the Epistle to the Hebrews. The general opinion seems to be that they were Jews who spoke Greek, lived outside of Palestine, and had been converted to Christianity. On account of this conversion they were persecuted by the orthodox Jews, and were in danger of losing their faith. The Epistle was written to show these Christians the superiority of their faith over the worn-out orthodoxy of Judaism, and to encourage them in maintaining their integrity. There has also been much controversy as to the authorship of the Epistle. Canon Farrar declares for Apollos, Kitto

for Paul, and other writers of equal authority for Luke, Mark, Silas, Barnabas and others. The evidences in support of the authorship of any one else than Paul, seem very dim and uncertain. The following are a few of the main peculiarities in the Epistle, which go to show that Paul was its author, because the same peculiarities appear in Paul's acknowledged Epistles: 1. The superiority of Christianity over Judaism. 2. The divine glory of Jesus after His self-humiliation on this earth. 3. Christ's sacrifice for man's sins, as prefigured in the Jewish sacrifices. 4. The condition of man's personal acceptance with God. The same figures of speech are used as in Paul's other Epistles: as, the *milk* and *meat* of doctrine, afflictions as a *contest*, or *strife*, Christian life, a *race*, etc. Lastly, many of the peculiarities of Paul's style, and certain allusions to the condition of the writer, corresponding to that of Paul, are of frequent occurrence throughout the Epistle. For these and other reasons we are safe in asserting that Paul was the author of the Epistle to the Hebrews, and that he wrote it toward the close of his two-years' stay in Rome, or about the year 64.

7. This is one of the noblest and most important of the Epistles of Paul, and will repay careful reading. In the first three chapters the dignity and majesty of Messiah as the Son of God are emphasized, as also His superiority over the angels and over Moses, through whom their primitive religion was revealed to the Jews. Therefore, Paul reasons, the religion of Christ is superior to Judaism. The High Priesthood of Christ is vindicated and compared to that of Melchizedek: the nature of this Priesthood being clearly detailed. (Chapters 4-7.) In chapters 8-10 the new covenant, the Gospel of Christ, is spoken of as the perfect fulfillment of the type found in the old covenant, the Law of Moses. This leads to the beautiful treatise on faith, contained in the 11th chapter. The remainder of the Epistle is taken up with exhortation and encouragement for the saints to hold fast to the faith, enduring any kind or degree of suffering in preference to giving way to sin or apostasy.

## REVIEW.

1. Why are the Epistles to Timothy and Titus called pastoral? 2. Who was Timothy? 3. What seems to have been his general character? 4. What was Paul's object in writing the First Epistle to Timothy? 5. The second? 6. Show by chapter 1 of the first Epistle the universality of the Gospel. 7. What duties of men are detailed in chapter 2? 8. What duties of women? 9. Name the chief qualifications of bishops, given in chapter 3. 10. Those of deacons. 11. What remarkable prophecy is recorded in chapter 4? 12. What personal exhortations to Timothy occur in this chapter? 13. What instructions in chapter 5 regarding the treatment of widows? 14. What instructions regarding the duties of servants are given in the 6th chapter? 15. How does Paul rebuke preaching for hire, in this chapter? 16. What personal exhortations occur in the second Epistle? 17. What evidences of the apostasy appear in chapter 3? 18. Ex-

plain chapter 4. verse 3. 19. How does Paul, in this chapter, speak of his coming death? 20. Give a brief account of the life of Titus. 21. What was Paul's object in writing to him? 22. What exhortations occur in the first chapter? 23. What duties of aged men and women are detailed in the second? 24. What duties of wives? 25. Of young men? 26. Of servants? 27. What general instructions in the 3d chapter? 28. Who are addressed in the Epistle to the Hebrews? 29. Why do we believe that Paul wrote this Epistle? 30. When and where did he write it? 31. What is said of Jesus in the first three chapters? 32. How is the Gospel compared with Judaism? 33. What does he say of Christ's Priesthood in chapters 4-7. 34. What relationship between the old and the new covenant is shown in chapters 8-10? 35. Quote passages on Faith from chapter 11. 36. What exhortation occurs in the remainder of the Epistle?

# LESSON XVII.

## THE CATHOLIC EPISTLES.

[I and II Peter: I John: and the Epistles of James and Jude.] *Note 1.*

| THE AUTHOR. | REFERENCES. |
|---|---|
| 1. Peter: birth, parentage, and early life. *Note 2.* | John 1: 42; 21: 16. |
| 2. Call to the ministry. *Note 3.* | John 1: 35-42. Matt. 4: 18. |
| 3. President of the church. (Primacy of Peter, James and John.) *Note 4.* | Matt. 16: 17-19. John 21: 15-18. |
| 4. His death at Rome. *Notes 5-6.* | John 21: 18-19. |
| 5. Character. *Note 7.* | John 1: 40-42. Matt. 16: 21-23. John 6: 66-69. Matt. 19: 27-28. Matt. 26: 31-35. Luke 22: 31-34. John 18: 10-12. |
| 6. The first Epistle of Peter. | |
|    a. Authorship. *Note 8.* | Eusebius, book III, chapter 2. |
|    b. Where written. *Note 9.* | Eusebius, book II, chapter 15. |
|    c. When written. *Note 10.* | |
| 7. Analysis. | |
|    a. To whom addressed: "Strangers," i. e. Gentiles, and Saints throughout Asia Minor. | I Peter 1: 2-3. |
|    b. Blessedness of the hope in Christ—an exhortation to holiness. | I Peter 1: 3-25; 2: 1-25; and 3: 1-16. |

    *c.* The preaching of Christ to the spirits in prison.    I Peter 3: 17-21.
    *d.* Object of such preaching. *Note 11.*    I Peter 4: 6.
    *e.* The spirit in which presiding elders are to exercise their authority. *Note 12.*    I Peter 5: 1-10.

**8. The second Epistle.**
    *a.* Authorship — canonicity questioned. *Note 13.*
    *b.* When written. *Note 14.*

**9. Analysis.**
    *a.* To whom addressed—"To them that have obtained like precious Faith," i. e., the Saints generally.
    *b.* Steps in the growth of righteousness.
    *c.* Peter's testimony to Christ's divinity.
    *d.* Prophecy of the apostacy.
    *e.* Warning of coming judgments—the earth destroyed by fire.
    *f.* A new heaven and earth.
    *g.* Exhortation.

## NOTES.

1. The descriptive title of this group of letters—The Catholic Epistles—is given them because they are not addressed to any church or person in particular, but to several communities; and in the case of I John and II Peter, apparently to the church universal. They differ in this particular from the letters of Paul, which are addressed to particular churches, to pastors, or to individuals named, except the Epistle to the Hebrews, and even that is addressed to a particular people. Generally II and III John are enumerated among the Catholic Epistles, but clearly this is a wrong classification, for they are decidedly personal letters, the second being addressed "unto the elect lady and her children" (II John 1.), possibly the wife and children of the writer; and the second is addressed to the "well beloved Gaius." For these reasons we do not include them in the group of Catholic Epistles. It should be noted that those who regard II John as

a "Catholic" Epistle, hold that the "elect lady," to whom the letter is addressed, is the church, and "her children," the members of the church.

2. But little is known concerning the early life of Peter. It is evident, however, that he was the son of a certain Jonas, or John, hence he is called in the scriptures, Simon Bar-jona (Matt. 16: 17). He was most probably a native of Bethsaida, in Galilee. With his brother Andrew he followed the occupation of fisherman on the sea of Galilee; and before they knew Jesus it is pretty certain that they were disciples of John the Baptist.

3. The first reference (John 1: 35-42) most likely gives the account of how Peter was first made acquainted with the Lord; the second evidently gives an account of a circumstance that occurred subsequent to Peter and Andrew's first meeting with Jesus, and may more properly be regarded as the call to the ministry. Peter was well advanced in middle life when that event occurred.

4. Whether the presidency of the church, as we now know it, was organized after the ascension of Jesus is a little uncertain. But that such an organization was discussed by Jesus and the Apostles is quite evident from the circumstance related of the mother of Zebedee's children (Matt. 20: 20-30). "Grant," said she to the Master, "that these my two sons, may sit, the one on thy right hand, and the other on the left, in thy kingdom." Evidently there had been something said that gave this woman and her sons, both of whom were of the Twelve, the idea that two of the number would be raised to the dignity here indicated, and that led this ambitious woman and her two sons to aspire to it. Jesus sought to dissuade them from their quest, but they stoutly affirming that they could endure the test he intimated might fall upon them, he at last plainly told them that it was not his prerogative to say who should sit on his right hand and who upon his left, but that it should be given to them for whom it had been prepared of his Father (verse 23).

But, however uncertain it may be about the organization of the First Presidency of the church, as we now know it, there can certainly be no question that Peter, James, and John enjoyed a certain primacy even during the life time of Jesus. This is evident from the fact that they were with Jesus in the mount of Transfiguration, when he received special ministration from Moses and Elias. These three also were separated from their brethren at the time of his suffering in the Garden, and seemed on various occasions to constitute a sort of inner council which the Lord gathered about him. That circumstance goes far towards confirming the likelihood of the existence of a First Presidency of three; and this likelihood is very much increased when one remembers that it was Peter, James, and John who restored the keys of the holy Apostleship to Joseph Smith in this dispensation.

5. It is well known that there is a diversity of opinion as to Peter's connection with Rome. Some deny that Peter ever was in Rome; others maintain that if he ever was there it was not until the last year of his life:

while others insist that he, with Paul, founded the church at Rome and resided there from twenty to twenty-five years. While there may be some ground for questioning the time at which Peter arrived at Rome, and some uncertainty as to just what part he took in founding the church at Rome, there is no good ground for disputing his presence in the city of the Cæsars: and even those who say he took no part in founding the church there are under the necessity of explaining away such authorities as the following: Eusebius in his Second Book, writing of the period between A. D. 41-54, describes how Simon Magus after being reproved at Samaria by Peter, fled to Rome where he established himself, taught his heresies, and practiced his magic—then adds: "This, however, did not continue long; for immediately under the reign of Claudius, by the benign and gracious providence of God, Peter, that powerful and great Apostle, who, by his courage, took the lead of all the rest, was conducted to Rome against this pest of mankind. He, like a noble commander of God, fortified with divine armor, bore the precious merchandise of the revealed light from the east to the west, announcing the light itself, and salutary doctrine of the soul, the proclamation of the Kingdom of God." (Eusebius Ecclesiastical History book 2, chapter 14.) Then again the same writer, quoting Dionysius, bishop of Corinth, represents him as saying in an address to the Romans: "Thus, likewise, you, by means of this admonition, have mingled the flourishing seed that had been planted by Peter and Paul at Rome and Corinth. For both of these having planted us at Corinth, likewise instructed us; and having in like manner taught in Italy, they suffered martyrdom about the same time." (Euseb. book 4, chapter 23. Dionysius flourished about the year A. D. 170.)

6. We have no account in the New Testament writings of the death of Peter. The reference above given concerning his death is the prophetic description of it by Jesus. Early Christian tradition relates that he was crucified at Rome during the Neronian persecution. "When the persecution began," it is said, "the Christians at Rome, anxious to preserve their great teacher, persuaded him to flee, a course which they had Scriptural warrant to recommend, and he to follow; but at the gate he met our Lord. 'Lord, whither goest Thou?' asked the Apostle. 'I go to Rome,' was the answer, 'there once more to be crucified.' Peter well understood the meaning of the words, returned at once and was crucified." (Smith's Dictionary of the Bible, Hackett's edition, Vol. 3, page 2454). The same work on the authority of Origen says that at his own request he was crucified with his head downward, and adds: "This statement was generally received by Christian antiquity; nor does it seem inconsistent with the fervent temperament and deep humility of the Apostle to have chosen such a death: one moreover, not unlikely to have been inflicted in mockery by the instruments of Nero's wanton and ingenious cruelty."—*Ibid.*

7. The character of Peter seems to be a strange blending of wonderful strength and astonishing weakness, with the former, however, predominant. Looking upon the weak side alone of his character, we are aston-

ished that he stood so high in the estimation of his Master; but throw into the opposite scale of the balance his strength of character and the wonder disappears. His weakness appears to have sprung from the impulsiveness and impetuosity of his nature and over confidence in his native strength. Weaknesses which time, that brings experience, was bound to correct and yet leave the strength of soul unimpaired. It was but natural that such a character as Peter should say when the Savior foretold his own sufferings at Jerusalem, his crucifixion and resurrection· "Be it far from Thee, Lord; this shall not be unto Thee." * It seems natural for a man of Peter's character when the Lord stood before him girt with a towel and ready to kneel and wash his feet, to stretch forth his hand and say: "Lord thou shalt never wash my feet." And equally natural for the same man to say when informed that unless the Master washed his feet he could have no lot nor part with him—"Lord not my feet only, but my head and my hands." We would expect Peter to say, when Jesus told the Twelve on the night of his betrayal, that they should all be offended because of him, "Though all men shall be offended because of Thee, yet will I never be offended." And when told that before the cock should crow he would thrice deny the Lord, we are scarcely surprised to see his spirit rise in its self-confidence, and scouting the Lord's prophetic power, say: "Though I should die with thee, yet will I not deny thee." But the time has now come for the wood, hay, and stubble of the man's character to be burned and the gold from the dross to be freed. This over self-confidence; this consciousness of personal strength and power, which up to this time Peter had doubtless referred to his own native strength of character, is to be smitten of God and destroyed. He is about to be taught the one great lesson that he needs to rid him of all his weakness of character and leave him revealed the "rock" which Jesus from the first knew him to be. The humiliation came. The spirit of the Lord withdrew. The man stands alone; thrice he denies the Lord, and emphasizes it with his blasphemies; receives the gentle look of reproof from the denied Lord, more terrible than thundered anathema to him, and with heart cleft in twain and all his self-confidence struck into the dust at his feet, he gropes his way into the darkness to weep and beat the earth in his shame. From this time the weakness disappears. Peter henceforth knows the true source of strength and constancy. He knows however strong man may be in and of himself—and some are strong and constant by nature, and among men there is wide difference in the possession of those qualities, which in the aggregate make up what we call strength—yet he needs God's power and God's strength to eke out his; to make him equal to all the emergencies that may arise within the experience of a servant of God. Peter so strengthened, will be able to say to the council of the Jews, who forbid him to speak or minister in the

---

* Language which called forth the severest reproof that Jesus ministered to any of his disciples so far as known: "Get thee behind me, Satan; thou art an offence unto me; for thou savorest not the things that be of God, but those that be of men." (Matt. 16: 22-23).

name of Messiah: "Whether it be right in the sight of God to hearken unto you more than unto God, judge ye. For we cannot but speak the things which we have seen and heard." (Acts 4: 19-20). And later, when a second time brought before the angry council, throwing aside all fear, yet with scourging and perhaps death in prospect he boldly said, when asked why he had violated the former injunction of the council: "We ought to obey God rather than man" (Acts 5: 29). And so throughout his subsequent noble ministry. His courage was equal to all trials, his constancy to all difficulties. Neither imprisonment nor death could daunt him; and when at last martyrdom did come he not only met it unflinchingly, but seemed even to voluntarily increase its horrors by asking that he be crucified head downward, deeming himself unworthy to be crucified as his Lord had been.

8. Authorship of the First Epistle. That Peter, the Apostle, was the author of the first epistle which bears his name, is confirmed by the voice of all early Christian tradition. "As to the writings of Peter," says Eusebius, "one of his Epistles called the first, is acknowledged as genuine. For this was anciently used by the ancient fathers in their writings, as an undoubted work of the Apostle" (Eusebius book III, chapter 1). "The internal evidence" says another authority, "is equally complete. The Author calls himself the Apostle Peter (chapter 1: 1), and the whole character of the Epistle shows that it proceeded from a writer who possessed great authority among those whom he addresses, who were composed chiefly of Jewish Christians. * * * The vehemence and energy of style are altogether appropriate to the warmth and zeal of Peter's character, and every succeeding critic, who has entered into its spirit, has felt impressed with the truth of the observation of Erasmus, 'that this Epistle is full of apostolical dignity and authority, and worthy of the prince of the apostles.' " (Biblical Literature—Kitto).

9. Where Written. The learned are very much divided as to the place where the First Epistle was written. The Author himself in closing the Epistle says: "The church which is at Babylon, elected together with you, saluteth you." By some it is held that this means simply that the Epistle was written at Babylon in Mesopotamia; while others, and especially Catholics, insist that "Babylon" is but the figurative name for Rome. The introduction to the First Epistle of Peter, in the Douay Bible, says: "He wrote it at Rome, which figuratively he calls Babylon." The other theory, viz., that it was written at Babylon on the Euphrates is not without the support of great scholars. It is maintained by "a host of learned men," says a good authority (Kitto), and "is a question which has never been, and probably. never will be decided;" and it is of no great moment whether it is decided or not.

10. The Epistle must have been written before A. D. 67-68, the year of St. Peter's martyrdom. Lardner places the date in A. D. 63 or 64, chiefly from the fact that an earlier date than A. D. 63, can not be assigned for his arrival at Rome. Hug and DeWette (introductions), and Neander

(History of the planting of the Christian Church). find an indication of the true date in the Neronian persecution, to which the Epistle manifestly refers. The Christians were now suffering persecution as Christians, and according to the popular belief, of which Tacitus informs us Nero took advantage, they were punished as evildoers. (Biblical-Literature—Kitto.)

11. For a brief treatment of the subject. Salvation for the Dead, clearly implied by the words of Peter respecting the matter of preaching to departed spirits. the student is referred to Roberts' "The Gospel," chapter 33.

12. following from the Doctrine and Covenants is in strict harmony with the ideas found in the references: Behold, there are many called, but few are chosen. And why are they not chosen? Because their hearts are set so much upon the things of this world. and aspire to the honors of men, that they do not learn this one lesson—that the rights of the Priesthood are inseparably connected with the powers of heaven, and that the powers of heaven cannot be controlled nor handled only upon the principles of righteousness. That they may be conferred upon us, it is true; but when we undertake to cover our sins, or to gratify our pride, our vain ambition. or to exercise control. or dominion, or compulsion, upon the souls of the children of men, in any degree of unrighteouness. behold. the heavens withdraw themselves. the Spirit of the Lord is grieved; and when it is withdrawn, Amen to the Priesthood or the authority of that man. Behold! ere he is aware. he is left unto himself, to kick against the pricks: to persecute the saints, and to fight against God. We have learned, by sad experience, that it is the nature and disposition of almost all men, as soon as they get a little authority. as they suppose. they will immediately begin to exercise unrighteous dominion. Hence, many are called, but few are chosen. No power or influence can. or ought to be, maintained by virtue of the Priesthood, only by persuasion. by long suffering, by gentleness and meakness, and by love unfeigned; by kindness and pure knowledge, which shall greatly enlarge the soul without hypocrisy. and without guile. Reproving betimes with sharpness. when moved upon by the Holy Ghost, and then showing forth afterwards an increase of love toward him, whom thou hast reproved, lest he esteem thee to be his enemy. (Doctrine and Covenants. section 121: 34-43).

13. The authenticity of the Second Epistle of Peter is a question too large to discuss in a brief note. Those who would become acquainted with a brief exposition of the *pros* and *cons* of the question cannot do better. perhaps, than to consult the article in Kitto's Biblical Literature. Here we can only say that both Catholic and Protestant writers very generally accept the tradition that the Apostle Peter was its author; but it cannot be denied that in very early times his authorship of it was questioned. Eusebius says of it: "But that which is called the second. we have not indeed understood to be embodied with the sacred books, yet as it appeared useful to many. it was studiously read with the other scriptures." The translator of Eusebius here quoted. C. F. Cruse, A. M., has the following

note on this passage: "That this Second Epistle of St. Peter was not at first received in the church of Christ with so universal agreement and consent as the former,' may be concluded from this passage in Eusebius. But, notwithstanding, there are great and sure evidences of this Epistle being written by the acknowledged author of it; as: 1. The title of Simon Peter, with the addition of 'an Apostle of Jesus Christ' (chap. 1:1.) 2. There is a whole passage in this Epistle (chap. 1: 16-17) which doth signally belong to Peter, that of having been on the holy mount with Christ, and hearing those words. 'This is my beloved Son.' etc., which certainly belongs to the transfiguration, (Matt. 17) where only Peter and James and John were present with Christ. 3. This is said to be a Second Epistle, (chap. 3: 1) written much to the same purpose with the former. 4. St. Jude, speaking (ver. 18) 'of the scoffers that should come.' etc., cites that prediction from 'the apostles of our Lord Jesus,' (ver. 17) where it is reasonable to believe that this Epistle (chap. 3: 3) is referred to; for in it those very words are met with (and are not so in any other apostolic writing) 'knowing this first.' etc. (Compare Jude 17-18 with II Peter 3: 3.) All this in all copies stands unmoved to secure the authority of this Epistle, and to convince us of the author of it." (See also Dr. Hammond's preface to the Second Epistle of Peter.)

14. By those who acknowledge its genuineness its date is generally fixed about the year A. D. 65, or not long before Peter's death, which they deduce from II Peter 1: 14. Wetstein concludes from II Peter 3, that it must have been written before the destruction of Jerusalem, in which case none will allege that any but Peter could have been its author. If it were proved that Peter had Jude's Epistle before him, this must have been written not long before the same period, which agrees with the time assigned by Dr. Lardner, between 64 and 66. *Biblical Literature.* (*Kitto.*)

## REVIEW.

1. Name the Catholic Epistles. 2. Why are they so called? 3. Why may II and III John be omitted from the list? 4. Give an account of the early life of Peter. 5. Of whom was he doubtless a disciple before he met Jesus? 6. Relate his call to the ministry. 7. What position in the church did Peter hold after Christ's death? 8. Who were associated with him? 9. What evidence have we that they were the First Presidency? 10. On what occasion during the life of Jesus had they been favored of Him? 11. What work did they perform in this dispensation? 12. What evidence have we that Peter was for a time in Rome? 13. What does Eusebius say of his contact with Simon Magus? 14. Where did Peter's death occur? 15. How is he believed to have been put to death? 16. Why did he not escape from the city (according to tradition)? 17. What elements of weakness were in Peter's character? 18. What elements of strength? 19. Relate instances to illustrate his impulsiveness. 20. What change in Peter occurred after Christ's death? 21. What instance illustrates his boldness?

22. Why do we conclude that Peter wrote the Epistles that bear his name? 23. What opinions are held as to where the First Epistle was written? 24. When was it written? 25. To whom was it addressed? 26. What does Peter say regarding the blessedness of the hope in Christ? 27. What exhortation occurs in the first three chapters? 28. Explain I Peter 3: 17-21. 29. What was the object of Messiah's preaching to the spirits in prison? 30. In what spirit are presiding Elders told to exercise their authority? 31. What is said in the Doctrine and Covenants regarding this matter? 32. Why is doubt cast on Peter's authorship of the Second Epistle? 33. What reasons have we for believing that he wrote it? 34. When was it written? 35. To whom is it addressed? 36. What steps in the growth of righteousness are outlined? 37. What testimony to Christ's divinity is borne? 38. Briefly state Peter's prophecy of the apostacy. 39. What changes in heaven and earth are predicted?

# LESSON XVIII.

## THE CATHOLIC EPISTLES. (Continued.)

| EPISTLES AND AUTHORS. | REFERENCES. |
|---|---|
| **1. The Epistle of James.** | |
|   *a.* By whom written. *Note 1.* | |
|   *b.* To whom addressed. *Note 2.* | |
|   *c.* When written. *Note 3.* | |
|   *d.* Its canonicity. *Note 4.* | |
|   *e.* Its occasion and object. *Note 5.* | |
|   *f.* Analysis. | |
|     Need of wisdom in temptation. | James 1: 1-18. |
|     Not hearers only, but doers. *Note 6.* | James 1: 19-27. |
|     Equality of rich and poor. | James 2: 1-13. |
|     Works with faith. *Note 7.* | James 2: 14-26. |
|     Control of the tongue. | James 3. |
|     Repentance and humility. | James 4. |
|     Woe to the proud and sinful. *Note 8.* | James 5: 1-6. |
|     Exhortation to faithfulness. | James 5: 7-20. |
| **2. The Epistle of Jude.** | |
|   *a.* To whom addressed. *Note 9.* | |
|   *b.* Its canonicity. *Note 10.* | |
|   *c.* Analysis. | |
|     His readers urged to contend for the faith, against ungodly teachers. | Jude 2-4. |
|     Reference to former sinfulness. | Jude 5-11. |
|     Judgment to come upon all sinners. | Jude 12-16. |
|     Contest between these and the faithful servants of God. | Jude 17-25. |

## NOTES.

1. It is not definitely known who wrote this epistle. So great is the doubt on this point that the epistle has been ascribed to three different men, James, the son of Zebedee and brother of John; James, the less, son of Alphaeus, and, like the son of Zebedee, an apostle; and James, the brother of our Lord, supposed to have been the first bishop of Jerusalem.

2. This was a catholic epistle, i. e., addressed to the church generally, and not to any particular branch. Some writers suppose it to have been addressed especially to the Jewish Christians, as distinguished from Gentile converts, but the only passage in support of this idea is the first verse, where the "twelve tribes" are addressed. This, however, may as well have reference to all Christians, who by accepting Christ were adopted into the house of Israel.

3. The date of this epistle is in considerable doubt. From internal evidence it has been maintained, though not definitely proved, that the epistle was written about the year 60, A. D.

4. By the canonicity of an epistle is meant its admission or rejection as a part of the Bible canon. In this respect, the Epistle of James has had a peculiar history. As early as the fourth century Eusebius referred to it in rather a doubtful way, and it was not until the year 397 that the Council of Carthage admitted it into the canon as the work of James, though it had been generally accepted by the churches earlier in the century. It was referred to as authentic by many prominent commentators up to the fifteenth century, when, during the progress of the reformation, its authenticity was first seriously attacked. Erasmus and Luther were the chief persons of note who called the epistle into question at that time. Their principal ground for attack was the fact that in this epistle the doctrine of works is taught, in apparent, but not real, contradiction of Paul's justification by faith. Salvation by faith was a favorite doctrine with Luther and his followers, and on this account many of them rejected the epistle of James. Most of the other reformers, among them the Calvinists accepted the epistle without question, and defended it against attacks. But the fact that the epistle was generally accepted as a part of the canon, and ascribed to James, is sufficient to establish its authenticity, while the high standing and authority of its writer renders it worthy of first place in a doctrinal sense. It is as worthy of our regard as any of the epistles of Paul. Yet, there is no definite evidence that the two great writers, Paul and James, were endeavoring to refute each other's works. Says Canon Farrar: "That Paul and James approached the great truths of Christianity from different points of view; that they did not adopt the same phrases in describing them; that they differed about various questions of theory and practice; even that they stood at the head of parties whose mutual bitterness they would have been the first to deplore—is clear from the Acts of the Apostles, and still more clear from scattered notices in the Epistles of Paul. But it is

quite common for the adherents of great thinkers to exaggerate their differences, and fail to catch their spirit. Whatever may have been the tone of the Jerusalem Pharisees towards Gentile Christians who paid no regard to the ceremonial law, we have the evidence of Paul himself (Gal. 2: 9; Acts 15: 13-21; 21: 17-25) as well as of public records of the church, that between him and the other Apostles there reigned a spirit of mutual respect and mutual concession. The view, therefore, that James was trying, in the approved modern fashion, to write down Paul, may be finally dismissed."

5. The occasion of this epistle seems to have been the growth of numerous and serious sins in the church; and the object of James in writing it was doubtless to rebuke and correct this tendency. In doing this James writes forcibly and boldly, as one who not only possessed authority, but was willing and able to use it in the interest of righteousness, and in the correction of false doctrine. There is no chance to misconstrue his statements or to consider him lacking in authority and force.

6. That the practical epistle of James is, in common with all other scripture, to be made use of in a practical way, is shown by the result of Joseph Smith's use of 1: 5. By interpreting the passage literally and asking for wisdom, he opened the way for the dispensation of the fullness of times.

7. On this subject, faith and works, the epistle has been very bitterly attacked by the protestant denominations. Yet this is one of the main reasons for the value of the epistle to the Latter-day Saints. The reasoning and the good sense displayed in this part of the epistle commend it to the favorable consideration of all who look upon religion as a matter of acts as well as professions.

8. This note of warning to the proud and sinful is one of the strongest denunciations of iniquity, in the scriptures. The successive sins are detailed with graphic force and clearness, and the judgments to follow are vividly depicted.

9. The epistle of Jude was addressed to the entire church, and was called forth, no doubt, by the rise of licentiousness in the church, and the necessity of warning the Christians against giving way to sinfulness. Attention is called to the judgments of God pronounced upon immoral peoples in the past, and by illustrations, exhortation, and reproof, Jude warns his readers to turn from darkness to the light.

10. The authenticity of this epistle as a production of one in authority, and therefore justified in promulgating the word of God, has never in modern times been called into serious question.

## REVIEW.

1. To what three writers is the epistle of James attributed? 2. To whom was it addressed? 3. When is it supposed to have been written? 4. What is meant by the canonicity of an epistle? 5. What authorities

have questioned the authority of the Epistle of James? 6. On what grounds? 7. Why do we accept the epistle? 8. In what important respect does it differ from some of Paul's epistles? 9. Show that this was not the result of any rivalry. 10. What was the occasion of writing the epistle? 11. What can you say of the forcible style of the epistle? 12. What passage in it is of especial interest to the Latter-day Saints? 13. Repeat this passage. 14. What practical features appear in the epistle? 15. What is James's idea of the relationship between rich and poor? 16. What is his doctrine of faith and works? 17. Why has this doctrine been opposed by some of the protestants? 18. Why do we commend it? 19. What warning is given in the last chapter? 20. To whom was the epistle of Jude addressed? 21. What do we think of its authenticity? 22. With what exhortation does it open? 23. What warnings are given? 24. With whom are the sinful contrasted?

## LESSON XIX.

## THE CATHOLIC EPISTLES—(Concluded.)

## THE EPISTLE OF JOHN.

THE WRITER OF THE EPISTLE. *Note 1.*  REFERENCES.

1. John the Apostle, (the Disciple whom Jesus loved). — Matt. 4: 21, Matt. 27: 56; compare with Mark 15: 40 and 16: 1.

   *a.* Parentage and early life. *Note 2.*

   *b.* Disciple of John the Baptist. *Note 3.* — John 1: 35-39.

   *c.* Becomes a disciple of Jesus, and also one of the twelve apostles. — John 1: 35-39. Matt. 10: 2. Luke 6: 12-14.

2. During Ministry in life time of Jesus.

   *a.* With Peter and James seems to form inner council with the Lord. — Mark 5: 37, Matt. 17: 1, Mark 13: 3, Matt. 26: 36-37.

   *b.* With James receives the descriptive name "Boanerges." — Mark 3: 17.

   *c.* Would call down fire from heaven on those who receive not the Lord. — Luke 9: 54.

   *d.* With James, his brother, seeks to be counsellor to our Lord in the heavenly kingdom. — Matt. 20: 20-24. Mark 10: 35-41.

   *e.* With Jesus in Gethsemane and at the house of the high priest after his apprehension. — Matt. 26: 36-38. John 18: 12-16.

   *f.* Follows Jesus to the cross and receives into his care the mother of our Lord. — St. John 19: 25-27.

3. After Resurrection of the Lord.

   *a.* Is prominent with Peter in work of the church. — Acts 3, Acts 4. Acts 8: 14-17.

4. **The later history of John as stated or implied in New Testament.**
 *a.* Driven by persecution to Patmos.   Rev. 1: 9.
 *b.* Seven churches of Asia under his peculiar care.   Rev. 1: 11 and Rev. chapters 2 and 3.
 *c.* In his ministry encountered men within the church who denied the truth.   I. John 4: 1, II. John 7.
 And also viciously denied his authority.   III. John 9: 10.
 *d.* John did not die, but remained God's witness in the earth. *Note 4.*   John 21: 20. John 25, Rev. 10: 8-11, Doc & Cov. Sec. 7.
5. **The character of John.**   *Note 5.*   Mark 3: 17, Matt. 20: 20-24, Mark 10: 35-41, Luke 9: 54.

**THE EPISTLE.**
6. **Where written.**   *Note 6.*
7. **When written.**   *Note 7.*
8. **Analysis:**
 *a.* The assurance that the writer had that Jesus is the Christ.   I. John 1: 1-4.
 *b.* Sinfulness of man, and forgiveness through Jesus Christ.   I. John 1: 6-10.
 *c.* The test by which we may know if men know God.   I. John 2: 3-6.
 *d.* Danger in love of the world.   I. John 2: 15-17.
 *e.* The warning concerning the coming of anti-Christ.   I. John 2: 18-23.
 *f.* The power imparted to the Saints to know all things and overcome.   I. John 2: 20-27.
 *g.* Manifestation of the love of God in that the faithful are called the sons of God. *Note 8.*   I. John 3: 1-3.
 *h.* Love the sign of having passed from death to life.   I. John 3: 13-24.
 *i.* The rival spirits of truth and error.   I. John 4: 1-6.

*j*. The principle of Christian life—
Love in God and in us.     I. John 4: 7-21.

*k*. The power of this love.     I. John 5: 1-12.

*l*. Christian confidence and assurance — "Little children—keep yourselves from idols."     I. John 5: 13:21.

## NOTES.

1. We may say that the unbroken voice of early Christian tradition accredits this Epistle to John. the apostle of the Lord, the author of the fourth Gospel and the Apocalypse. This tradition is the chief reason for accounting John the apostle as its author. Next to the evidence of that tradition is the identity of its doctrine and the style of its composition with the doctrine and style of the fourth Gospel. Certain expressions and mannerisms throughout proclaim that the author of one of these books is certainly the writer of the other; and therefore whatever testimony exists tending to prove that the "disciple whom Jesus loved" wrote the fourth gospel may also be relied upon as proving that he wrote the First Epistle of John. With this identity of doctrine and style referred to in mind, we recommend the reading of both the Epistle and the fourth Gospel together for the purpose of identifying the points of comparison in the general structure of the composition, in style of expression, and in doctrine.

2. As with nearly all the New Testament characters so with John, but very little is known of his early life. The date of his birth is uncertain, but it is generally believed that he was one of the youngest and indeed the very youngest of our Lord's disciples among the apostles: certainly younger than his brother James, whose name is always coupled with his wherever the names of the Twelve are enumerated, and most likely younger than Jesus himself. His father was a fisherman of Bethsaida of the name of Zebedaeus or Zebedee (Matthew 4: 21), of whom we know nothing further. "The traditions of the fourth century," says the writer *on this subject in Smith's dictionary of the Bible, "make his mother, Salome, the daughter of Joseph [the husband of Mary, who was the mother of Christ] by his first wife, and consequently half sister to our Lord. By some recent critics she has been identified with the sister of Mary the mother of Jesus in John 19: 25. They lived, it may be inferred from John 1: 44, in or near the same town [Bethsaida] as those who were afterwards the companions and partners of their children. There on the shores of the Sea of Galilee, the apostle and his brother [James] grew up. The mention of the "hired servants" (Mark 1: 20), of his mother's "substance" (Luke 8: 3), of "his own house" (John 19: 27), implies a position removed at least some steps from absolute poverty. The fact that the apostle was

―――――――
*This is Edward H. Plumptre, M. A., Professor of Divinity in King's College, London. Smith's Dict. Bible (Hackett) Vol. II., page 1420.

known to the high priest Caiaphas, as that knowledge was hardly likely to have begun after he had avowed himself the disciple of Jesus of Nazareth, suggests the probability of some early intimacy between the two men or their families."

3. That John the Apostle was a disciple of John the Baptist is based chiefly upon the supposition that the unnamed one of the two disciples mentioned in John 1: 40, was John; Andrew, Simon Peter's brother, being the other. "Assuming that the unnamed disciple of John 1: 37-40 was the evangelist himself, we are led to think of that meeting, of the lengthened interview that followed it, as the starting-point of the entire devotion of heart and soul which lasted through his whole life." (Smith's Dict. of Bib., Vol. II., p. 1421.)

4. The fate of John is an interesting theme, and one of very great uncertainty as will appear from the quotation which follows from "Early Days of Christianity" by Canon Farrar: "Respecting the death of St. John we are left in the completest darkness. The words: "slew with the sword" suffice to record the martyrdom of his elder brother: not one word tells us how the last, and in some respects the greatest, of the apostles passed to his reward. It is only a very late and worthless rumor which says that he was killed by the Jews. From the silence of all the early fathers as to his supposed martyrdom, we may assume it for certain, that so far as they knew, he died quietly at Ephesus in extreme old age. His grave was shown at Ephesus for several centuries, and the legend that the dust was seen to move with the breathing of the great apostle as he lay in immortal sleep, arose from the awe with which it was regarded. But the age which he attained—far surpassing, if some of our accounts are true, the ordinary three score years and ten—only deepens the impression that he would not die till Christ returned. He did not die till Christ had returned, in that sense the 'close of the Aeon' to which his own words and that of his apostles often point; but legend said that he had been taken alive to heaven like Enoch and Elijah, and that sometimes he still wandered and appeared on earth. So prevalent were such notions as to his immortality, even during his life time, that in the appendix to his Gospel he thought it necessary to point out the erroneous report of the words of Jesus from which they had been inferred." Early Days of Christianity pp 403-4. The references in the analysis, however, furnish sufficient proof that John did not die: on the contrary he was appointed to remain as God's witness in the earth until the glorious appearing of the Lord Jesus in the clouds of heaven and in the glory of his Father. A similar privilege was accorded to three of the twelve apostles on the western hemisphere. The circumstance of their obtaining that peculiar privilege is quoted here as it is directly connected with this incident in the life of John. The three Nephite apostles received the privilege alluded to above during the ministry of Jesus on this western hemisphere after his resurrection from the dead, and it is thus related in the Book of Mormon: "And it came to pass when Jesus had said these words, he spake unto his disciples, one by one.

saying unto them. 'What is it that ye desire of me, after that I am gone to the Father?' And they all spake, save it were three: 'We desire that after we have lived unto the age of man, that our ministry, wherein thou hast called us, may have an end, that we may speedily come unto thee, in thy kingdom.' And he said unto them, 'Blessed are ye, because ye desire this thing of me; therefore after that ye are seventy and two years old, ye shall come unto me in my kingdom, and with me ye shall find rest.' And when he had spoken unto them, he turned himself unto the three, and said unto them, 'What will ye that I should do unto you, when I am gone unto my Father?' And they sorrowed in their hearts, for they durst not speak unto him the thing which they desired. And he said unto them, 'Behold, I know your thoughts, and ye have desired that thing which John, my beloved, who was with me in my ministry, before that I was lifted up by the Jews, desired of me; therefore more blessed are ye, for ye shall never taste of death, but ye shall live to behold all the things of the Father, unto the children of men, even until all things shall be fulfilled, according to the will of the Father, when I shall come in my glory, with the powers of heaven; and ye shall never endure the pains of death; but when I shall come in my glory, ye shall be changed in the twinkling of an eye from mortality to immortality; and then shall ye be blessed in the kingdom of my Father. And again, ye shall not have pain while ye shall dwell in the flesh, neither sorrow, save it be for the sins of the world; and all this will I do because of the thing which ye have desired of me, for ye have desired that ye might bring the souls of men unto me, while the world shall stand.'" *Book of Mormon, III Nephi 28: 1-9.*

5. We are apt to think of John as a character almost effeminate because of the emphasis which in all his writings he places upon love; because, perhaps, of the fact that he is several times referred to as the "disciple whom Jesus loved;" because of the influence of early Christian art which always represents him as gentle, yielding, and effeminate, a characterization sustained by much of early Christian tradition. And doubtless he was of gentle mien and temper, one of those natures in which sweetness predominates, who proceeds by persuasion rather than by argument; by statement and testimony of the truth, rather than by debate; and who wins by expression and proof of love, rather than by attempts to convince the reason and hold the judgment. But after all this is admitted, it must not be thought that his gentleness degenerated into weakness; or that because he was emphatically the apostle of love he lacked force. The fact that Jesus bestowed upon him and his brother James the name "Boanerges," that is, sons of thunder, would alone be sufficient to correct such an error. The further fact that he and his brother James were ready to call down thunder and destroy the Samaritans who rejected the message of the Lord; and that he and James aspired to be the counselors to the Lord in the Heavenly Kingdom, while one smacks of over zeal and narrow conceptions of the Master's mission, and the other approaches dangerously near an inordinate ambition,—at least have their virtue that they

correct the idea that John was of so retiring, modest and gentle disposition as to be weak or effeminate. He doubtless was a man of kind nature, loving and gentle disposition, but at bottom fearless, bold, determined, and strong.

6. Place of writing the First Epistle.—On this head nothing certain can be determined. It has been conjectured by many interpreters, ancient and modern, that it was written at the same place as the Gospel. The more ancient tradition places the writing of the Gospel at Ephesus, and a less authentic report refers it to the island of Patmos. Hug (Introduction) infers, from the absence of writing materials (III John 13), that all John's Epistles were composed at Patmos. The most probable opinion is that it was written somewhere in Asia Minor, in which was the ordinary residence of the apostle (Euseb. Hist. Eccl. iii. 23), perhaps, according to the tradition of the Greek church, at Ephesus; but for this we have no historical warrant (Lucke's Commentary).

7. The age of the Epistle.—It is difficult to determine the time of the writing of this epistle, although it was most probably posterior to the Gospel, which seems to be referred to in 1. John i. 4. Some are of the opinion that the epistle was an envelope or accompaniment to the gospel, and that they were consequently written nearly simultaneously (Hug's Introd.). As, however, the period when the Gospel was written, according to the evidence of tradition and criticism, "fluctuates between the sixth and ninth decennium of the first century" (Lucke's Comment.), we are at a loss for data on which to found any probable hypothesis respecting the exact time of the writing of the epistle; but that it was posterior to the Gospel is further rendered probable from the fact that it is formed on such a view of the person of Jesus as is found only in St. John's Gospel, and that it abounds in allusion to the speeches of Jesus, as there recorded.

8. This passage—1. John 3: 1-3—clearer perhaps than any other affirms the relationship between God and men—the relationship of Father and sons. "Now are we the sons of God; and it doth not yet appear what we shall be"—that is, our full development is not yet known, the intelligence, the wisdom, the power, the glory, the honor are not within our conception —"but we know that when he [i. e. Christ] shall appear, we shall be like Him. * * * * And every man that hath this hope in him purifieth himself, even as he [Christ] is pure." For further remarks on this passage and the general theme it suggests, see "New Witness for God," ch. 30.

## REVIEW.

1. Who was the writer of this epistle? 2. Who was his father? 3. What was his vocation? 4. Give an account of his early life. 5. What was the financial condition of the family? 6. Why do we think John was a disciple of John the Baptist? 7. Give an account of his becoming a follower of Jesus. 8. Who were with him at the time? 9. What traits in John's character are made most prominent in the Gospels? 10. Why do we think he was not weak? 11. Relate incidents to illustrate his

strength of character. 12. How was he associated with Peter and James? 13. What incidents in Christ's life did these three alone witness? 14. What charge was given to John at the death of Jesus? 15. How was he associated with Peter and James after the resurrection of Jesus? 16. What incidents occurred in John's later life? 17. How do we know that he did not die? 18. What other personages are to live till Christ comes again? 19. Relate the incident. 20. What is known regarding the time and place of writing the epistle? 21. What assurance does John give that Jesus is the Christ? 22. How only may man obtain forgiveness of sin? 23. What test is given to determine whether men know God? 24. What danger is pointed out in the love of the world? 25. What warning is given concerning the coming of anti-Christ? 26. What power was spoken of as being given to the Saints? 27. How is the sonship of man to God spoken of? 28. What prominence is given to the principle of love? 29. What is John's closing admonition?

## LESSON XX.

## THE APOCALYPSE.

We cannot persuade ourselves that a study of the Apostolic Age would be complete without some consideration being given to what may be regarded as the most wonderful, and at the same time, the most instructive book produced in that age, viz.: The Apocalypse or Book of Revelation, written, beyond all question, by the Apostle John. Latter-day Saints should have a double interest in that book for the reason that through the revelations given to the Prophet Joseph Smith, they may know more both about its author and about the book itself, than others who believe in its authenticity. And yet it is to be feared that they very much neglect their advantages in respect to this subject.

Now as to the first, viz: knowledge of the author. In the writings of the first Nephi, it is recorded that the Lord revealed to him very many things both as to the past and the future, some of which he recorded, and others he was forbidden to write of, because the privilege of doing so was reserved to another, viz: to John the Apostle. Following is the passage: "And it came to pass that the angel spake unto me, saying, Look! And I looked and beheld a man, and he was dressed in a white robe; and the angel said unto me, Behold one of the Twelve Apostles of the Lamb! Behold he shall see and write the remainder of these things; yea, and also many things which have been; and he shall also write concerning the end of the world; wherefore, the things which he shall write, are just and true; and behold they are written in the book which thou hast beheld proceeding out of the mouth of the Jew; and at the time they proceeded out of the mouth of the Jew, or at the time the book proceeded out of the mouth of the Jew, the things which were written, were plain and pure, and most precious, and easy to the understanding of all men. And behold, the things which this Apostle of the Lamb shall write, are many things which thou hast seen; and behold, the remainder shalt thou see, but the things which thou shalt see hereafter, thou shalt not write; for the Lord God hath ordained the Apostle of the Lamb of God, that he shall write them. And also others who have been, to them hath he shown all things, and they have written them; and they are sealed up to come forth in their purity, according to the truth which is in the Lamb, in the own due time of the Lord, unto the house of Israel. And I, Nephi, heard and bear record, that the name of the Apostle of the Lamb was *John*, according to the word of the angel." (Book of Mormon, I Nephi 14: 18-27).

As to the *second*, viz: the book itself. The Prophet Joseph Smith, at Hiram, Portage County, Ohio, about the 1st of March, 1832, gave a key to John's Revelations, the whole of which is respectfully commended to the attention of the student, but from which we make the following quotation, on which the analysis to follow, by Elder B. H. Roberts, is based.

Q—What are we to understand by the book which John saw, which was sealed on the back with seven seals?

A—We are to understand that it contains the revealed will, mysteries, and works of God; the hidden things of his economy concerning this earth during the seven thousand years of its continuance, or its temporal existence.

Q—What are we to understand by the seven seals with which it was sealed?

A—We are to understand that the first seal contains the things of the first thousand years, and the second also of the second thousand years, and so on until the seventh. * * * * * * *

Q—What are we to understand by the sounding of the trumpets, mentioned in the eighth chapter of Revelation?

A—We are to understand that as God made the world in six days, and on the seventh day he finished his work, and sanctified it, and also formed man out of the dust of the earth; even so, in the beginning of the seventh thousand years will the Lord God sanctify the earth, and complete the salvation of man, and judge all things, and shall redeem all things, except that which he hath not put into his power, when he shall have sealed all things, unto the end of all things, and the sounding of the trumpets of the seven angels, are the preparing and finishing of his work, in the beginning of the seventh thousand years—the preparing of the way before the time of his coming. (Doctrine and Covenants, section 77).

The writer of the analysis hopes to enter into a thorough exposition of the book of Revelation as soon as his literary engagements will admit of it. Meantime he commends to the attention of the student the analysis he has prepared. After the preface to the Revelation—a preface which clearly shows the handwork of John—compare with preface to the Gospel according to St. John—and the message to the seven churches of Asia, then commences the great compendium of the political history of the world through the seven thousand years of its temporal existence; and in this connection we suggest that the student take any standard history and by dividing the history into periods of a thousand years, he will be both instructed and astonished by the accuracy with which the sacred writer has symbolized these periods. The prophetic political history of the earth is followed by the prophetic ecclesiastical history—but the analysis will speak for itself; and only needs careful consideration to demonstrate the Apocalypse as one of the most remarkable, as well as one of the most instructive, books in the sacred collection.

## REVIEW.

1. What book in the New Testament is known as the Apocalypse? 2. By whom was it written? 3. Where was the revelation given to him? 4. About when was it given? 5. Relate Nephi's vision of John the Revelator. 6. How may the Latter-day Saints gain a full knowledge of the Book of Revelation? 7. What did the book which John saw contain? 8. What were the seven seals? 9. What is meant by the sounding of the trumpets? 10. In what order was the revelation given? 11. Under what circumstances was it given to John? 12. What key is given as to the time the Book of Revelation covers? 13. What seven churches in Asia are addressed by John? 14. What evidences of the approaching apostacy are recorded in chapters 2-4? 15. How is the first period of a thousand years symbolized? 16. What condition prevailed during this period? 17. How is the second period symbolized? 18. What condition then prevailed? 19. Give symbol and condition of the third period. 20. Of the fourth. 21. Of the fifth. 22. Of the sixth. 23. Of the seventh. 24. In which of the periods are we living? 25. What five periods of church history are prophetically recorded? 26. In which of these periods are we living? 27. What are the four divisions of Part IV? 28. With what beautiful description does this part close? 29. What evidence against the divinity of the Book of Mormon do sectarians try to find from Rev. 22:18? 30. Show that it contains no such proof.

# LESSON XXI.

## CLOSE OF THE FIRST CENTURY A. D.   *Note 1.*

### EVENTS.   (A. D. 66-100.)

1. Date, Place and Manner of Paul's Death. *Note 2.*
2. Date, Place and Manner of Peter's Death. *Note 3.*
3. Later History of John. *Note 4.*
4. Condition of the Church at the Close of the Century. *Note 5.*

### NOTES.

1. The consecutive scriptural history of the Christian era ends with the account of Paul's arrival and two years' stay in Rome, or about 64 A. D. For the history of the other church leaders before that time, and of these and Paul to the close of the first century, we depend largely upon occasional allusions in the Epistles and the Apocalypse, and on the writings, more or less traditional, of the early Christian fathers. Out of this mass of tradition, a few statements have stood out with great distinctness, and have been pronounced more or less reliable. These will be stated in this lesson, in order to supplement the account given in the Acts, and round out the history of the church for the first century. A caution is here urged, that the facts here presented are not entirely free from theories and baseless tradition, and should, therefore, be accepted with great caution. It is also necessary that no doctrinal ideas shall be based upon them; these must depend upon the authentic truths of scripture, both ancient and modern.

2. After Paul's arrival at Rome, about 62 A. D., he remained there two years, being allowed sufficient liberty to visit the Christians and minister to them. At the close of this imprisonment he is said to have been permitted to leave Rome for a time and visit the branches of the church in Greece and Asia Minor, and some authorities state that he traveled as far west as Spain and Britain. He is then supposed to have returned to Rome, about 65, though the exact year is not known. It was during the reign of

the tyrant Nero. The Christians were in great disfavor with this emperor, and he was making the destruction of Rome by fire, in the year 64, an excuse for treating them with severe cruelty. They were put to death in many ways, the manner of their suffering being graphically described by Canon Farrar: "Imagine that awful scene, once witnessed by the silent obelisk in the square before St. Peter's at Rome! Imagine it, that we may realize how vast is the change which Christianity has wrought in the feelings of mankind! There, where the vast dome now rises, were once the gardens of Nero. They were thronged with gay crowds, among whom the emperor moved in his frivolous degradation—and on every side were men dying slowly on their cross of shame. Along the paths of those gardens on the autumn nights were ghastly torches, blackening the ground beneath them with streams of sulphurous pitch, and each of those living torches was a martyr in his shirt of fire. And in the ampitheatre hard by, in sight of twenty thousand spectators, famished dogs were tearing to pieces some of the best and purest of men and women, hideously disguised in the skins of bears or wolves." Tradition asserts that during this long-continued Neronian persecution, Paul met his death, probably about the year 66. He was slain "with the sword," we suppose by beheading.

3. So far as the account given in the Acts of the Apostles is concerned, we lose sight of Peter at a very early period. But by a reference in Galatians 2: 11, we are given a little further knowledge regarding him, viz., that he labored in Antioch. After this, his life is shrouded in the mists of tradition. One of these traditions is to the effect that he wrote his First Epistle from Babylon, and acted for a time as Bishop of Antioch. All early traditional accounts seem to agree that he was martyred at Rome, by order of Nero, about the year 67. That he met his death by crucifixion, is indicated by the prophecy of Christ recorded in John 21: 18-19, as well as by tradition. Says Kitto: "Another tradition reports the Apostle (Peter) as having toward the close of his life visited Rome, become bishop of the church in that city, and suffered martyrdom in the persecution raised against the Christians by Nero. The importance of these points in connection with the claims urged by the Catholics on behalf of the supremacy of the pope, has led to a careful and sifting examination of the accuracy of this tradition, the result of which seems to be that whilst it is admitted as *certain* that Peter suffered martyrdom, in all probability by crucifixion, and as *probable* that this took place at Rome, it has, nevertheless, been made pretty clear that he never was, for any length of time, resident in that city, and morally certain that he never was bishop of the church there." This certainty that Peter never was bishop of Rome, is further confirmed by the fact that he was an Apostle; and the two offices, the Apostleship and the Bishopric, are very different. The one is a general office, the other local; one is spiritual, the other temporal; one pertains to the Melchizedek priesthood, the other, in its literal meaning, to the Aaronic. Therefore, it is most unreasonable to suppose that Peter stepped down from the high dignity of the Apostleship, where he exercised authority

over the whole church, to the more humble position of a bishop, where his authority would be exercised over only a portion of the church, even though it were so important a portion as the See of Rome.

4. John also drops out of our knowledge at an early date, so far as the book of Acts is concerned. Nor can very much be gleaned from his Epistles or the Revelation, regarding his subsequent life. But according to Paul's statement, (Gal. 2: 9) John was in Jerusalem, and one of the "pillars" of the church, when, about 50 A. D., the question of circumcising Gentile converts was decided. Nothing more is heard of him until about eighteen years later, he was banished to the Isle of Patmos, in the Aegean Sea, where he received and wrote the Revelation. Two legends related of him are to the effect that he was thrown into a cauldron of boiling oil, and given a poisoned cup, escaping unharmed from both dangers; but these appear to be doubtful. It is quite certain that he spent some years at Ephesus, and according to some authorities it was at this city that he wrote his Epistles, the last books of the Bible canon written (about 96 A. D.)

5. At the close of the first century, the church was in a sadly demoralized condition. According to our best authorities, all the Apostles but John were dead, no attempt having been made to maintain the quorum. If so important a body was allowed to become extinct, there is no reasonable doubt that other quorums fell into decay and that the Church organization lost its original identity. With the disorganization of the quorums of Priesthood there was an opportunity for the predicted rise of false teachers under whom occurred changes in the ordinances of the Gospel. These changes afterward increased materially until, in connection with the loss of true, and the usurpation of false authority, they produced a complete change both in the organization and the ordinances of the church. Persecution and internal corruption and dissension had also done their work, until at the close of the century, when John wrote his Epistles and the Revelation, but few of the branches of the church retained enough of their identity and faithfulness to be recognized by him. The deplorable condition of the church can well be gathered from the warnings and threats given to the saints at Ephesus in the second chapter of Revelation. A full discussion of this subject will be found in Roberts' New Witness for God, chapters 2-7. From the evidences there presented, it cannot be doubted that at the close of the first century the high authority of the church had fallen into decay, and the Apostolic Age was at an end.

## REVIEW.

1. Up to what year does the account in the Acts bring the history of the church? 2. From what sources are other items of church history gathered? 3. What can you say of the reliability of these sources? 4. What was Paul's employment during his first two years in Rome? 5. What visits is he said to have made subsequently? 6. What persecutions were occurring in Rome at Paul's return? 7. How were the Christians put to death? 8. How is Paul said to have been martyred? 9. In what year?

10. What is the last mention of Peter in the New Testament? 11. What labors is he said to have performed after this time? 12. How was he martyred? 13. Where did this occur? 14. In what year? 15. Discuss the claim that Peter was Bishop of Rome? 16. Name the later events in the life of John. 17. How do we know that he did not die? 18. What conditions of apostacy developed toward the close of the first century? 19. What was the condition of the church at the close of the century? 20. Why was the Apostolic Age at an end at this time?

www.ingramcontent.com/pod-product-compliance
Lightning Source LLC
Chambersburg PA
CBHW031604110426
42742CB00037B/1110